MICROWAVE COOKING FOR TODAY'S LIVING

PHOTO CREDITS:

Royal Copenhagen Porcelain Corporation, 683 Madison Avenue, New York, NY 10021-porcelain, glassware and stainless flatware.

Georg Jensen Silversmiths, 683 Madison Avenue, N.Y.C. 10021, sterling silver.

Schott-Zwiesel Glass Inc., 11 East 26th St., N.Y.C. 10010, crystal and glassware.

The Pottery Barn, 213 Tenth Ave., N.Y.C. 10011, & Manhattan Ad Hoc Housewares, 842 Lexington Ave., N.Y.C. 10021, miscellaneous pottery and housewares.

D. Porthault, 57 East 57th St., N.Y.C. 10022, table linens.

TABLE OF **CONTENTS**

INTRODUCTION

1. HOW YOUR MICROWAVE OVEN WORKS

Microwaves are a form of energy similar to radio and television waves and to ordinary daylight. Everything emits microwaves—the kitchen sink, a coffee pot, even people—but ordinarily microwaves spread outward as they travel through the atmosphere and disappear without effect. Our microwave oven, however, is constructed in such a way as to take advantage of microwave energy. Electricity is converted into microwave energy by the magnetron tube, and microwaves are then sent into the cooking area through openings at the top of the oven. A turntable is located at the bottom of the oven.

Microwaves cannot pass through the metal walls of the oven, but they can penetrate such materials as glass, porcelain, paper, and wicker, the materials out of which microwave-safe cooking dishes are constructed. Microwaves do not heat the cookware, through cooking vessels will eventually get hot from the heat generated by the food. Rather, microwaves are attracted to the moisture in foods and cause the water molecules to vibrate, 2,450 million times per second. As the water molecules vibrate they rub against each other, producing friction. This friction, in turn, causes the food to heat. If you have trouble imagining how this is possible, just think how hot your hands would get if you rubbed your palms together 2,450 million times per second!

A very safe appliance: Your Microwave oven is one of the safest of all home appliances. When the door is opened, the oven automatically stops producing microwaves. Although microwave ovens have been in operation in American kitchens since the mid-1950s, according to government reports there has yet to result even one injury from their use. And by the way, by the time microwave energy has been converted into heat in the process of making your food hot, the microwaves are completely spent. Thus, there is no "residue" of any kind in food that has been cooked by microwaves.

2. GETTING THE BEST RESULTS WITH YOUR MICROWAVE OVEN

Keeping an eye on things: The recipes in this book have been formulated with great care, but your success in preparing them depends, of course, on how much attention you pay to the food as it cooks. Always watch your food as it cooks. Your microwave oven is equipped with a light that turns on automatically when the oven is in operation so that you can see inside and check the progress of your recipe.

Directions given in recipes to "elevate," "stir," "rotate," and the like should be thought of as the minimum steps recommended. If the food seems to you to be cooking unevenly, do whatever you think necessary to correct the problem.

Factors affecting cooking times: The cooking times given in the recipes in this book are approximate rather than exact. Many factors affect cooking times. The temperature of ingredients used in a recipe makes a big difference in cooking times.

For example, a cake made with ice-cold butter, milk, and eggs will take considerably longer to bake than one made with ingredients that are at room temperature. Another important factor in determining cooking times is the strength and intensity of your house current. The house power of homes in some rural communities is considerably stronger than the power available to the dwellers in many cities. The stronger your house power, the more quickly your food will cook.

You should also keep in mind that on very cold or very hot days, a great deal of electricity is diverted for heating or cooling. Thus less electricity is available to your oven, and the oven will cook more slowly than usual.

Range of cooking times: All of the recipes in this book give a range of cooking times. In general, you will find that the food remains undercooked at the lower end of the time range, and you may sometimes.

Reflection   *Transmission*   *Absorption*

want to cook your food beyond the maximum time given. Personal preferences vary, as do the cooking speeds of different ovens under different conditions. The governing philosophy is this book is that it is best for a recipe to be conservative in giving cooking times, for while undercooked food may always be cooked a bit more, overcooked food is ruined for good.

Some of the recipes, particularly those for breads, cakes, and custards recommend that the foods be removed from the oven when they are still slightly undercooked. This is not a mistake. When allowed to stand, usually covered, these foods will continue to cook outside of the oven as the heat trapped within the outer portions of the foods gradually travels inward. If the foods are left in the oven until they are cooked all the way through, the outer portions will become overcooked or even burnt. As you gain experience in using your microwave oven, you will become increasingly skillful in estimating both cooking and standing times for various foods.

3. HOW CHARACTERISTICS OF FOODS AFFECT MICROWAVE COOKING

Density of foods: Light, porous food such as cakes and breads cook more quickly than heavy, dense foods such as roasts and casseroles. You must take care when microwaving porous foods that the outer edges do not become dry and brittle. Shield edges with foil or microwave at a low power level.

Height of foods: The upper portion of tall foods, particularly roasts, will cook more quickly than the lower portion. Therefore, it is wise to turn tall foods during cooking, sometimes several times.

Moisture content of foods: Since microwaves are attracted by moisture, relatively dry foods such as roasts and some vegetables should either be sprinkled with water prior to cooking or covered so as to retain steam.

Bone and fat content of foods: Bones conduct heat, and large amounts of fat attract microwave energy. Therefore, care must be taken when cooking bony or fatty cuts of meat that the meats do not cook unevenly and do not become overdone.

Quantity of foods: The number of microwaves in your oven remains constant regardless of how much food is being cooked. Therefore, the more food you place in the oven, the longer the cooking time. Remember to decrease cooking times by at least one-third when halving a recipe.

Shape of foods: Microwaves penetrate only about 1 inch into foods; the interior portion of thick foods is cooked as the heat generated on the outside travels inward. In other words, only the outer inch of any food is actually cooked by microwave energy; the rest is cooked by convection. It follows, then, that the worst possible shape for a food that is to be microwaved is a thick square: the corners will burn long before the center is even warm. Round, thin foods and ring-shaped foods microwave the most successfully.

Size of foods: The smaller and more uniform the pieces of food in the oven, the better. It is also a good idea to microwave cut-up foods in a roomy pan so that the microwaves can get to the pieces from all sides, thus ensuring even cooking.

4. SPECIAL TECHNIQUES IN MICROWAVE COOKING

Browning: Meats and poultry that are cooked fifteen minutes or longer will brown lightly in their own fat. Foods that are cooked for a shorter period of time may be brushed with a browning sauce to achieve an appetizing color.

The most commonly used browning sauces are Worcestershire sauce, soy sauce, barbecue sauce and concentrated meat broth. Since relatively small amounts of browning sauces are added to foods, the original flavors of recipes are not altered.

Covering: A cover traps heat and steam and causes food to cook more quickly. You may either use a lid or a sheet of plastic wrap with a corner folded back to prevent splitting.

Covering with wax paper: Wax paper effectively prevents food from spattering and helps food to retain some heat. But because wax paper makes a looser cover than a lid or than plastic wrap, it allows food to dry out slightly.

Wrapping in wax paper or paper towel: Sandwiches and many other foods containing prebaked bread should be wrapped prior to microwaving to prevent drying out.

Arranging and spacing: Individual foods such as baked potatoes, cupcakes, and hors d'oeuvres will heat more evenly if placed in the oven an equal distance apart, preferably in a circular pattern. Never stack foods on top of one another.

Stirring: Stirring is one of the most important of all microwaving techniques. In conventional cooking, foods are stirred for the purpose of blending. Microwaved foods, however, are stirred in order to spread and redistribute heat. Always stir from the outside toward the center, as the outside of foods heats first.

Turning over: Large, tall foods such as roasts and whole chickens should be turned so that the top and bottom will cook evenly. It is also a good idea to turn cut-up chicken and chops.

Placing thicker portions facing outward: Since microwaves are attracted to the outside portion of foods, it makes sense to place thicker portions of meat, poultry, and fish facing the edge of the baking dish. This way, thicker portions will receive the most microwave energy and the foods will cook evenly.

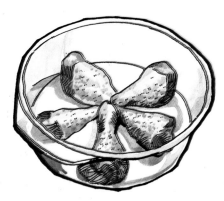

Shielding: Strips of aluminum foil, which block microwaves, are sometimes placed over the corners or edges of square- and rectangular-shaped foods to prevent those portions from overcooking. Never use too much foil, and make sure the foil is tightly secured to dish, or else you may cause the oven to "flash".

Elevating: Thick or dense foods are often elevated so that microwaves can be absorbed by the underside and center of the foods.

Piercing: Foods enclosed in a shell, skin, or membrane are likely to burst in the oven unless they are pierced prior to cooking. Such foods include both the yolks and whites of eggs, clams and oysters, and many whole vegetables and fruits.

Testing for doneness: Because foods cook so quickly in a microwave oven, it is necessary to test for doneness frequently. Some foods are left in the microwave oven until completely cooked, but most foods, including meats and poultry, are removed from the oven while still slightly undercooked and allowed to finish cooking during standing time. The internal temperature of foods will rise between 5 °F and 15 °F during standing time.

Standing time: Foods are often allowed to stand for 3 to 10 minutes after being removed from the microwave oven. Usually the foods are covered during standing time to retain heat, unless they are supposed to be dry in texture (some cakes and cookies, for example). Standing allows foods to finish cooking and also helps flavors to blend and develop.

5. MICROWAVE-SAFE UTENSILS

Never use metal or metal-trimmed utensils in your microwave oven. Microwaves cannot penetrate metal. They will bounce off any metal object in the oven—just as they bounce off the metal walls of the oven—and cause "arcing", an alarming phenomenon that resembles lightning.

Most heat-resistant, nonmetallic cooking utensils are safe for use in your microwave oven. However, some may contain materials that render them unsuitable as microwave cookware. If you have any doubts about a particular utensil, there's a simple way to find out if it can be used in your microwave oven.

Testing utensils for microwave use: Place the utensil in question next to a glass measure filled with water in the microwave oven.
Microwave at power level HIGH for 1 minute. If the water heats up, but the utensil remains cool to the touch, the utensil is microwave-safe. However, if the water does not change temperature, but the utensil becomes warm, microwaves are being absorbed by the utensil and it is not safe for use in the microwave oven.

You probably have many items on hand in your kitchen right now that can be used as cooking equipment in your microwave oven. Read through the following checklist.

1. China plates: Many kinds of china are microwave-safe. If in doubt, consult the manufacturer's literature or perform the microwave test.

2. Glassware: Any glassware that is heat-resistant is microwave-safe. This would include all brands of oven-tempered glass cookware. Do not, however, use delicate tumblers, wine glasses, and the like in the oven, as these are likely to shatter as the food heats up.

3. Paper: Paper plates and containers are convenient and safe to use in your microwave oven, provided that the cooking time is short and the foods to be cooked are low in fat and moisture.
Paper towels are also very useful for wrapping foods and for lining baking trays in which greasy foods such as bacon are cooked. In general, avoid colored paper products, as the color may run.

4. Plastic storage containers: These can be used to hold foods that are to be quickly reheated. However, they should not be used to hold foods that will need considerable time in the oven, as hot foods will eventually warp or melt plastic containers.

5. Plastic cooking bags: Provided that they are made especially for cooking, plastic cooking bags are microwave-safe. However, be sure to make a slit in the bag so that steam can escape. Never use ordinary plastic bags for cooking in your microwave oven, as they will melt and rupture.

6. Plastic microwave cookware: A variety of shapes and sizes of microwave cookware is available. For the most part, you can probably microwave with items that you already have on hand rather than investing in new kitchen equipement. However, certain special items such as plastic ring modls and muffin tins are very convenient.

7. Pottery, stoneware, and ceramic: Containers made of these materials are usually fine for use in your microwave oven, but they should be tested to be sure.

8. Wicker, straw, wood, sea shells: All of these materials are safe for brief use in your microwave oven.

9. Metal utensils: Metal utensils and utensils with metal straps, clips, or screws should not be placed in your microwave oven while the oven is in operation, as they may cause arcing.
Metal skewers may be used in you microwave oven as long as they are well covered with food.
It is better, however, to use wooden skewers if possible. These are available at reasonable prices at most cookware shops.

Use these utensils

Do not use these utensils

6. SOME MICROWAVING TIPS

Boiling water: Place 1 cup water in a 2-cup glass measure and microwave, uncovered, at power level HIGH for 2½ to 3½ minutes.

Instant coffee: Place 6 ounces water in microwave-safe cup or mug. Microwave, uncovered, at power level HIGH for 2 to 2½ minutes, or until hot. Stir in coffee crystals. Handle of cup of mug will still be cool.

Hot cocoa: Place 1 to 2 teaspoons each cocoa powder and sugar in an 8-ounce mug. Gradually add 6 ounces milk or skim milk, stirring to blend. Microwave, uncovered, at power level HIGH for 2 to 2½ minutes, or until hot, stirring once. Watch carefully so that milk does not boil over.

Heating syrup or honey: Place in a glass pitcher and microwave, uncovered, at power level HIGH until warm. One cup syrup or honey will take about 3 minutes.

Melting butter or margarine: Place butter or margarine in a custard cup or glass measure. Microwave, uncovered, at power level LOW & DEFROST until melted. Two to four tablespoons will take between 2½ and 5 minutes. One to two sticks will take 5 to 9 minutes. Watch carefully to prevent burning.

Softening butter, margarine, or cream cheese: Unwrap and place on a serving plate. Microwave, uncovered, at power level LOW & DEFROST checking at 10-second intervals.

Melting chocolate squares and chocolate pieces: Place in a custard cup or glass bowl and microwave, uncovered, at power level LOW & DEFROST. One square unsweetened chocolate or 1 cup (6 ounces) chocolate pieces will take 4 to 5 minutes. Two squares unsweetened chocolate or 2 cups chocolate pieces will take 5 to 7 minutes. Stir to smooth.

Melting caramels: Combine 1 14-ounce package caramels and 2 tablespoons water in a 4-cup glass measure. Microwave, uncovered, at power level HIGH for 4 to 6½ minutes, or until melted, stirring every minute.

Toasting almonds: Place shaved or slivered almonds in a shallow baking dish and add 1 teaspoon butter or margarine per ½ cup nuts. Microwave, uncovered, at power level HIGH for 2½ to 5 minutes, depending on the amount. Stir every 30 seconds and watch closely.

Toasting coconut: Place unsweetened flaked or grated coconut in a shallow baking dish. Microwave, uncovered, at power level HIGH for about 3 minutes per cup. Stir every 30 seconds and watch closely to prevent burning.

Freshening stale chips and pretzels: Place chips or pretzels in a napkin-lined wicker basket. Microwave, uncovered, at power level HIGH for about 1 minute per cup, or until snacks feel warm. Let stand a few minutes to cool before serving.

Warming bread and rolls: Wrap in a napkin or place in a napkin-lined wicker basket and cover with a napkin. Microwave at power level HIGH just until bread or rolls feel warm.

Cooking bacon: Place bacon slices on a double thickness of paper toweling and cover with a paper towel. Microwave at power level HIGH for about 1¼ minutes per slice, or until crisp. If you wish to save the drippings, microwave bacon on a rack rather than on toweling.

7. PRECAUTIONS TO AVOID POSSIBLE EXPOSURE TO EXCESSIVE MICROWAVE ENERGY.

1. **Do not attempt to operate this oven with the door open** since open-door operation can result in harmful exposure to microwave energy.
It is important not to defeat or tamper with the safety interlocks.

2. **Do not place any object** between the oven front face and the door or allow soil or cleaner residue to accumulate on sealing surfaces.

3. **Do not operate the oven if it is damaged.** It is particularly important that the oven door close properly and that there is no damage to the:
   (1) door (bent)
   (2) hinges and latches (broken or loosened)
   (3) door seals and sealing surfaces.

4. **The oven should not be adjusted or repaired** by anyone except properly qualified service personnel.

APPETIZERS

Curried Chicken Balls
(Recipe on page 12)

CHICKEN LIVER PATE

1 pound chicken livers, halved
1 cup butter or margarine
½ cup finely chopped green onion
¼ cup dry sherry or chicken broth
1 clove garlic, pressed or finely chopped
¼ teaspoon ground thyme
pinch ground cloves or allspice
¾ teaspoon salt
¼ teaspoon pepper

1. Combine all ingredients in a 1½-quart glass casserole. Cover. Microwave at power level LOW & DEFROST for 19 to 24 minutes, or until liver is done to taste, stirring twice.
2. Pour mixture into blender or food processor and blend until smooth. Pour into serving container and cover securely. Chill until firm. Serve with crackers.

Makes about 2½ cups.

STUFFED MUSHROOMS

½ pound medium-size mushrooms

4 tablespoons butter or margarine
½ cup finely chopped green onion
3 tablespoons bread crumbs
1 tablespoon dried parsley flakes

1. Clean mushrooms and separate caps and stems. Arrange caps hollow-side-up in a single layer in a 10-inch round baking dish. Set aside.
2. Dice mushroom stems finely. Combine with butter and green onion in a 1-quart glass casserole. Microwave, uncovered, at power level HIGH for 4 to 5 minutes, or until onion is tender, stirring twice. Add bread crumbs and parsley flakes. Set aside.
3. Cover mushroom caps and microwave at power level HIGH for 2½ to 4 minutes, or until nearly cooked. Stuff each cap with some of the bread crumb mixture. Cover and microwave at power level HIGH for 2½ minutes, or until hot.

Makes 25 to 30 pieces.

SPICY SHRIMP

½ cup chili sauce
½ cup sweet pickle relish
½ cup beer
¼ teaspoon chili powder

½ pound medium shrimp, shelled and cleaned

1. Combine all ingredients except for shrimp in a 1-quart glass casserole. Set microwave oven at power level HIGH for 5 minutes, and then power level LOW & DEFROST for 16 minutes. Stir occasionally during cooking. The sauce should be hot and thickened.
2. Stir in shrimp, cover, and microwave at power level HIGH for 2½ to 3½ minutes, or until shrimp are curled, stirring once. Let stand, covered, 2 minutes. To serve, skewer with picks or pass with cocktail picks or toothpicks.

Makes about 1 cup.

POLYNESIAN SAUSAGE BITES

2 tablespoons brown sugar
1 tablespoon cornstarch
⅔ cup orange or pineapple juice
1 tablespoon soy sauce
1 clove garlic, pressed or finely chopped
¼ teaspoon ground ginger
dash cayenne pepper
½ pound brown-and-serve sausages

1. In a 2-quart glass casserole stir brown sugar and cornstarch together. Slowly add fruit juice, blending thoroughly to make a smooth paste. Stir in soy sauce, garlic, and seasoning. Cut sausages in ¾-inch pieces and fold them into sauce mixture.
2. Microwave at power level HIGH for 6 to 9 minutes, or until sauce is hot and thickened, stirring 2 or 3 times. Pass with cocktail picks or toothpicks.

Makes about 1½ cups.

WALNUT CHEESE WAFERS

1 8-ounce jar process cheese spread
6 tablespoons butter or margarine, softened
1¼ cups flour
pinch cayenne pepper

½ cup chopped walnuts

1. Blend cheese, butter, flour, and cayenne pepper until smooth. Divide mixture in half and place on two sheets of wax paper. Roll up to form 2 6-inch logs. Refrigerate until firm.
2. Unwrap logs and roll in chopped walnuts to coat. Cut each log into 24 ¼-inch pieces. Arrange 12 pieces in a circualr pattern on a paper plate. Microwave at power level LOW & DEFROST for 4½ to 6 minutes. Let stand 1 minute before removing from plate with spatula. Repeat procedure with remaining pieces.

Makes 48 wafers.

CRABMEAT PUFFS

¾ cup crabmeat (about 6 ounces)
½ cup mayonnaise
2 tablespoons finely chopped onion
1 teaspoon prepared mustard
1 teaspoon lemon juice

12 crisp crackers or rounds of melba toast

1. Drain crabmeat and combine well with all ingredients, except crackers or toast.
2. Mound crab mixture on the crackers or toast. Arrange 6 crackers in a circle on a glass or paper plate. Microwave, uncovered, at power level HIGH for 2 to 2½ minutes, or until puffed and very hot. Repeat procedure with remaining 6 crackers.

Makes 12 pieces.

SWEET AND SOUR TUNA CRACKERS

½ 7-ounce can tuna, well drained
4 tablespoons cream cheese, softened
3 tablespoons crushed pineapple, well drained
1 tablespoon white vinegar
⅛ teaspoon curry powder

24 crackers or melba toast rounds

1. Flake tuna and combine with all remaining ingredients, except crackers, in a 1-quart mixing bowl. Blend thoroughly.
2. Spread mixture on 24 crackers or melba toast rounds. Arrange 12 pieces in a circle on a paper plate. Microwave, uncovered, at power level HIGH for 2½ to 4 minutes, or until crackers are bubbing. Repeat procedure with remaining crackers.

Makes 24 pieces.

CURRIED CHICKEN BALLS

1½ cups finely minced cooked chicken
¼ cup mayonnaise
3 tablespoons finely chopped raisins
2 tablespoons dried onion flakes
2 tablespoons dried bread crumbs
1 teaspoon lemon juice
½ teaspoon curry powder

1 egg, lightly beaten
1 cup dried bread crumbs

1. Mix together all ingredients, except egg and the one cup of bread crumbs. Shape into 24 balls.
2. Dip balls in beaten egg and then roll in crumbs. Arrange 12 pieces in a circle on a paper plate and microwave, uncovered, at power level HIGH for 3 to 4 minutes, or until heated through. Repeat procedure with remaining 12 pieces. Serve with curry-flavored mayonnaise.

Makes 24 pieces.

CHILI DIP

½ pound ground beef
½ cup finely chopped onion

1 6-ounce can tomato paste
1 1¼-ounce envelope chili seasoning mix
1 clove garlic, pressed or finely chopped

1. Crumble beef into 1½-quart glass casserole. Add onions. Cover. Microwave at power level HIGH for 4 to 5 minutes, or until beef is browned, stirring once. Drain off fat.
2. Stir in tomato paste, chili seasoning, and garlic. Cover. Microwave at power level HIGH for 4 to 5 minutes, or until hot. Serve with corn chips.

Makes 2 cups.

CHEESY COCKTAIL SNACKS

4 tablespoons butter or margarine

2 cups bite-size, unsweetened breakfast cereal
1½ cups pretzel sticks
1 cup salted mixed nuts
1 envelope Italian salad dressing mix
¼ cup grated Parmesan cheese

1. Place butter or margarine in a 2-quart glass casserole and microwave, uncovered, at power level HIGH for 1½ to 2½ minutes, or until melted.
2. Add remaining ingredients and toss thoroughly. Microwave, uncovered, at power level LOW & DEFROST for 13 minutes, or until warmed, stirring 4 or 5 times.

Makes 4½ cups.

SEASONED COCKTAIL NUTS

8 ounces shelled nuts or unsalted canned nuts
1 tablespoon butter or margarine
2 teaspoons Worcestershire sauce
1 teaspoon salad seasoning
½ teaspoon garlic salt
¼ teaspoon celery salt
¼ teaspoon hot pepper sauce

1. Combine all ingredients in a 10-inch round baking dish.
2. Microwave, uncovered, at power level HIGH for 10 minutes, stirring 4 times. Cool on paper towels. Store in a tightly covered container.

Makes about 2 cups.

ESCARGOTS BOURGUIGNONNE

½ cup butter, softened
1 tablespoon finely chopped green onion
2 tablespoons finely chopped parsley
2 cloves garlic, pressed or finely chopped
⅛ teaspoon salt
⅛ teaspoon pepper

1 3-ounce can snails, drained, plus 12 snail shells
1 tablespoon dry bread crumbs

¼ cup white wine

1. In a small mixing bowl, beat butter, green onion, parsley, garlic, salt, and pepper to form a smooth paste.
2. Pleace a dab of the butter mixture in the bottom of each of 12 snail shells. Add the snails and fill the shells with remaining butter mixture. Sprinkle the opening of shells with bread crumbs.
3. Arrange snails in a circular pattern on a glass plate or baking dish. Pour white wine into bottom of baking dish. Microwave, uncovered, at power level LOW & DEFROST for 7½ to 10 minutes, or until butter is bubbling. Pass with toothpicks and serve French bread on the side.

Makes 12 snails.

SAUCES & DESSERT TOPPINGS

*Spaghetti Sauce
(Recipe on page 16)*

WHITE SAUCE

4 tablespoons butter or margarine
4 tablespoons flour
½ teaspoon salt
¼ teaspoon white pepper (optional)
2 cups milk

1. Place butter or margarine in a 1-quart glass bowl. Microwave, uncovered, at power level HIGH for 1½ to 2½ minutes, or until melted.
Stir in flour, salt, and pepper, making a smooth paste.
Gradually add milk, blending well.
2. Microwave, uncovered, at power level HIGH for 4½ to 6 minutes, or until sauce is thickened and bubbly, stirring occasionally.

Makes 2 cups.

VARIATIONS

Cheese sauce: Stir 1 to 1¼ cups shredded cheese (Cheddar, Swiss, Parmesan, or some combination of cheeses) into finished sauce. If necessary, microwave at power level HIGH for ½ minutes to melt cheese.
Curry sauce: Stir 2 to 4 teaspoons curry powder in along with flour.
Mustard sauce: Add 4 to 6 tablespoons prepared mustard to finished sauce. Season with dashes of Worcestershire sauce.

ONIONY CREAM SAUCE

1 11-ounce can condensed cream of onion soup
1 3-ounce package cream cheese
¼ cup white wine
2 tablespoons milk or cream
1 teaspoon instant beef bouillon
¼ teaspoon pepper

1. Combine all ingredients in a 1-quart glass bowl. Cover. Microwave at power level LOW & DEFROST for 6½ to 8 minutes, or until warm.
2. Beat mixture to blend well.
Microwave, uncovered, at power level HIGH for 2½ to 3½ minutes, or until hot, strring once.

Makes about 1¾ cups.

BASIC BROWN SAUCE

¼ cup finely chopped onion
4 tablespoons butter or margarine or meat drippings

3 tablespoons flour
1 11-ounce can beef broth
1 teaspoon tomato paste (optional)
¼ teaspoon salt
⅛ teaspoon pepper
⅛ teaspoon ground thyme

1. Combine onion and butter or meat drippings in a 1-quart glass bowl. Microwave, uncovered, at power level HIGH for 4 minutes, or until onion is softened, stirring once.
2. Stir flour into onion mixture. Gradually add beef broth, stirring to make sure there are no lumps. Add remaining ingredients. Microwave, uncovered, at power level HIGH for 4½ to 5½ minutes, or until thickened and bubbly, stirring twice.

Makes about 1½ cups.

CURRY-CHEESE SAUCE

1 11-ounce can condensed Cheddar cheese soup
1 teaspoon curry powder
¼ cup milk

1. In a 4-cup glass measure, beat soup and curry powder until thoroughly blended. Gradually add milk, beating to mix well.
2. Microwave, uncovered, at power level HIGH for 2½ to 4 minutes. or until hot, stirring twice. Serve over vegetables.

SPAGHETTI SAUCE

½ cup finely chopped onion
2 tablespoons oil, preferably olive oil

2 8-ounce cans tomato sauce
3 to 4 cloves garlic, pressed or finely
    chopped
1½ teaspoons basil or oregano
½ teaspoon salt
¼ teaspoon pepper

1. Combine onion and oil in a 1-quart glass bowl. Microwave, uncovered, at power level HIGH for 4 to 5 minutes, or until onion is fairly soft.
2. Add remaining ingredients. Cover. Set microwave oven at power level HIGH for 4 minutes, and then power level HIGH for 9 minutes. Stir 3 times.

Makes about 2 cups.

CREOLE SAUCE

½ cup finely chopped onion
¼ cup finely chopped green pepper
¼ cup finely chopped celery
2 tablespoons oil, preferably olive oil
2 cloves garlic, pressed or finely chopped
¼ to ½ teaspoon chili powder

1 15-ounce can tomato sauce

1. Combine all ingredients, except tomato sauce, in a 1½-quart glass bowl. Cover. Microwave at power level HIGH for 4 minutes, stirring once.
2. Stir in tomato sauce. Cover. Set microwave oven at power level HIGH for 6 minutes, and then at power level LOW & DEFROST for 11½ minutes. Stir once after 5 minutes.

Makes about 2½ cups.

QUICK HOLLANDAISE SAUCE

½ cup (1 stick) butter
1 egg, lightly beaten

2 tablespoons lemon juice
salt and pepper to taste

1. Place butter in a 2-cup glass measure and microwave at power level HIGH for 2½ to 4 minutes, or until melted. Beat in the egg, using a wire whip. Microwave, uncovered, at power level LOW & DEFROST for 1½ minutes, or until egg appears slightly set.
2. Beat in lemon juice, whisking briskly with wire whip to prevent lumps. Season to taste with salt and pepper. Use at once with fish or vegetables. Do not attempt to reheat.

Makes about ¾ cup.

BEARNAISE SAUCE

¼ cup finely chopped onion
1 tablespoon dried tarragon leaves
3 tablespoons white vinegar
¼ teaspoon salt
¼ teaspoon pepper

3 egg yolks

½ cup (1 stick) butter

1. Combine onion, tarragon, vinegar, salt, and pepper in a deep 1-quart glass bowl. Microwave, uncovered, at power level HIGH for 2½ minutes, stirring once. Let stand 2 minutes.
2. Whisk egg yolks into vinegar mixture, blending well. Microwave, uncovered, at power level LOW & DEFROST for 1½ minutes, or until mixture thickens, stirring every 30 seconds. Remove from oven and set aside.
3. Cut butter into pats and place in a 2-cup glass measure. Microwave at power level HIGH for 2½ to 4 minutes, or until melted and bubbling. Immediately begin pouring butter very slowly into reserved egg yolk mixture, whisking sauce constantly with wire whip or hand-held electric beater. The sauce should thicken as the butter is added, becoming a mayonnaise-like cream. Strain sauce if desired. Serve on meat or fish. Do not attempt to reheat.

Makes about 1 cup.

SWEET AND SOUR SAUCE

1 tablespoon cornstarch
½ cup packed dark brown sugar
¾ cup pineapple juice
½ cup cider vinegar
1 tablespoon soy sauce
½ cup finely chopped green pepper

1. Stir brown sugar and cornstarch together in a 1-quart glass bowl. Gradually add pineapple juice and stir mixture until completely smooth. Stir in remaining ingredients.
2. Microwave, uncovered, at power level HIGH for 4½ to 5½ minutes, or until sauce is bubbly and thickened, stirring 3 times.

Makes about 1¾ cups.

CUSTARD SAUCE

3 tablespoons sugar
2 tablespoons flour
1½ cups milk

2 egg yolks
1½ teaspoons vanilla extract

1. Mix sugar and flour together in a 1-quart glass bowl. Gradually add ¼ cup of the milk, stirring to make smooth paste. Add the remainder of the milk, beating to combine well. Microwave, uncovered, at power level HIGH for 4½ to 5½ minutes, or until sauce is bubbly and thickened, stirring every minute.
2. Using a wire whip, quickly whisk in both egg yolks. Microwave, uncovered, at power level LOW & DEFROST for 1½ to 2 minutes, or until sauce thickens, stirring every 30 seconds. Stir in vanilla extract.
Serve warm or chilled.

Makes about 1¾ cups.

VANILLA SAUCE

⅓ cup sugar
2 tablespoons cornstarch
1½ cups milk

1½ tablespoons butter or margarine
1 tablespoon vanilla extract

1. In a 1-quart glass bowl, stir sugar and cornstarch together. Gradually add enough of the milk to make a smooth paste. Stir in the remainder of the milk. Microwave, uncovered, at power level HIGH for 4½ to 5½ minutes, or until sauce is bubbly and thickened, stirring twice.
2. Stir in butter and vanilla extract. Serve warm or chilled over cake or fruit.

Makes about 1¾ cups.

LEMON PUDDING SAUCE

1 3¼-ounce package regular lemon pudding mix
½ cup sugar
1 teaspoon grated lemon peel
¼ teaspoon ground nutmeg
1¼ cups water
1 cup milk

1 tablespoon butter or margarine

1. In a 1½-quart glass bowl, stir together pudding mix, sugar, lemon peel, and nutmeg. Gradually add water, blending to make a smooth paste. Stir in the milk. Microwave, uncovered, at power level HIGH for 7½ to 9 minutes, or until mixture is thickened and bubbly, stirring every minute. At first, the sauce will look lumpy.
2. Beat in the butter until sauce is smooth. Serve warm over cake or fruit.

Makes about 2½ cups.

Cherry Sauce with Brandy
(Recipe on page 19)

CHERRY SAUCE WITH BRANDY

½ cup sugar
1½ tablespoons cornstarch
¼ cup brandy
1 tablespoon lemon juice (optional)
1 1-pound can pitted cherries in heavy
   syrup

1. Combine sugar and cornstarch in a 1-quart glass bowl. Gradually add brandy, stirring to make a smooth paste. Add lemon juice and cherries. Stir to blend well.
2. Cover bowl and microwave at power level HIGH for 10 to 13 minutes, or until sauce is hot and thickened, stirring twice. Serve warm over ice cream or cake.

Makes about 2½ cups.

Notes

SOUPS

Bouillabaisse
(Recipe on page 23)

OLD-FASHIONED CHICKEN SOUP

1¼ pounds chicken parts
2 ribs celery, cut into ½-inch lengths
2 carrots, scraped and cut into ½-inch
  lengths
1 onion, sliced
4 cups hot water
1 teaspoon salt
1 bay leaf
1 teaspoon peppercorns
½ teaspoon whole thyme leaves
1 small clove
2 chicken flavored bouillon cubes

½ to ¾ cup fine egg noodles

1. Place chicken parts, celery, carrot, onion, hot water, bouillon cubes and salt in a 2-quart glass casserole. Wrap bay leaves, peppercorns, thyme leaves, and clove in a square of washed cheesecloth or washed undyed cotton or linen. Tie herb bundle with string and add to casserole. Cover. Set microwave oven at power level HIGH for 15 minutes, and then power level LOW & DEFROST for 38 minutes.
2. Add noodles to soup. Cover. Microwave at power level LOW & DEFROST for 10 minutes. Let soup stand 8 to 10 minutes longer, or until noodles are completely tender. Remove chicken meat from bones before serving, if desired. Discard herb bundle.

Makes 3 to 4 servings.

CHICKEN GUMBO

1 pound chicken parts

1 cup sliced onion
1 tablespoon flour
1 16-ounce can stewed tomatoes
1 10-ounce package frozen okra, thawed
1 8-ounce can corn
2 cups chicken broth
1½ teaspoons salt
¼ teaspoon hot pepper sauce
¼ teaspoon pepper
⅛ teaspoon garlic powder

1. Arrange chicken pieces with their meatiest sides facing outward in a 3-quart glass casserole. Cover. Microwave at power level HIGH for 9 to 11½ minutes, or until chicken is cooked. Remove chicken from casserole and set aside to cool.
2. Add onion to casserole containing chicken juices. Microwave, uncovered, at power level HIGH for 4 minutes. Stir in flour. Add all remaining ingredients. Set microwave oven at power level HIGH for 9 minutes, and then power level LOW & DEFROST for 16 minutes. Stir 4 times.
3. While soup is cooking, remove chicken meat from bones. Add chicken meat to soup. Cover. Microwave at power level LOW & DEFROST for 8 minutes. Let stand 5 minutes.

Makes 5 to 6 servings.

HAWAIIAN CHICKEN SOUP

2 11-ounce cans condensed chicken noodle
  soup
1 10-ounce package frozen Hawaiian-style
  vegetables with pineapple
2 cups water
½ cup pineapple juice
1 teaspoon soy sauce

1. Combine all ingredients in a 2-quart glass bowl. Microwave, uncovered, at power level HIGH for 15 to 19 minutes, or until soup boils, stirring occasionally.
2. Microwave at power level LOW & DEFROST for an additional 4½ to 8 minutes, or until vegetables are tender.

Makes 4 to 5 servings.

CONSOMME MADRILENE

2 11-ounce cans condensed consomme
⅔ cup tomato juice
⅔ cup water
⅓ cup dry sherry
1 teaspoon lemon juice (optional)

1. Combine all ingredients in a 2-quart glass bowl. Stir to blend.
2. Microwave at power level HIGH for 7 to 9 minutes, or until hot, stirring twice. Serve, if desired, with sour cream and chopped parsley on top.

Makes 4 to 5 servings.

VEGETABLE SOUP

1 quart chicken broth
1 large onion, sliced
2 carrots, scraped and cut into ¼-inch
   rounds
2 medium potatoes, peeled and cut into
   ½-inch dice
3 stalks celery, cut into ¼-inch slices
2 tablespoons finely chopped parsley
1 teaspoon basil
½ teaspoon salt

1 large tomato, peeled, seeded, and cut into
   ½-inch chunks
1 cup frozen cut green beans, thawed
1 cup frozen peas, thawed
1 cup frozen cauliflower, thawed and cut up
1 to 2 cups torn lettuce or spinach leaves

1. Combine broth, onion, carrots, potatoes, celery, parsley, basil, and salt in a 3-quart glass casserole. Cover. Set microwave oven at power level HIGH for 9 minutes, and then power level HIGH for 10½ minutes.
2. Add remaining ingredients. Cover. Microwave at power level HIGH for 4½ to 7 minutes, or until all vegetables are tender.

Makes 6 to 8 servings.

MINESTRONE

4 tablespoons bacon drippings or oil,
   preferaly olive oil
½ cup thinly sliced onion
½ cup thinly sliced carrot

2 cups chicken broth
2 cups water
1 16-ounce can tomatoes, coarsely chopped
1 cup shredded cabbage or zucchini
1 to 2 cloves garlic, finely chopped
1 teaspoon basil or oregano
1 teaspoon dried parsley flakes
1 teaspoon salt
¼ teaspoon pepper

1 16-ounce can kidney beans, drained
½ cup frozen peas, thawed
⅓ cup spaghetti, broken into 2-inch pieces

1. In a 3-quart glass casserole, combine drippings or oil and onion and carrot. Microwave, uncovered, at power level HIGH for 6 to 7½ minutes, or until vegetables are beginning to brown lightly, stirring once.
2. Add broth, water, tomatoes, cabbage or zucchini, garlic, basil or oregano, parsley flakes, salt, and pepper. Cover. Microwave at power level HIGH for 10 minutes, stirring once.
3. Add remaining ingredients. Cover. Microwave at power level LOW & DEFROST for 16 to 19 minutes, or until vegetables are tender, stirring occasionally. Let stand, covered, for 5 to 10 minutes, or until spaghetti is tender.

Makes 4 servings.

VICHYSSOISE

4 tablespoons butter or margarine
3 large leeks, white part only, thinly sliced

1½ cups chicken broth
1½ cups milk
½ cup whipping cream
2 medium potatoes, peeled and shredded
big pinch ground thyme
big pinch ground nutmeg
¾ teaspoon salt
¼ teaspoon white pepper

1. Combine leeks and butter in a 2-quart glass bowl. Microwave, uncovered, at power level HIGH for 5 minutes, or until leeks are fairly soft, stirring twice.
2. Add all remaining ingredients. Cover. Set microwave oven at power level HIGH for 6 minutes, and then power level LOW & DEFROST for 24 minutes. Stir once after 3 minutes of cooking.
2. Puree soup in blender or food processor. Chill and serve sprinkled with snipped chives or parsley, or serve hot.

Makes 4 servings.

ONION SOUP

3 cups thinly sliced onions
4 tablespoons butter or margarine

3 11-ounce cans beef broth

slices of toasted French bread
1½ cups shredded Swiss cheese
¼ cup greated Parmesan cheese

1. Combine onions and butter in a 3-quart glass casserole. Microwave uncovered, at power level HIGH for 7½ to 10 minutes, or until onions are very soft, stirring twice.
2. Add beef broth and cover. Set microwave oven at power level HIGH for 5 minutes, and then power level HIGH for 9 minutes. Stir once after 3 minutes.
3. Ladle soup into 4 individual bowls. Cover with bread slices and sprinkle with the two cheeses. Microwave at power level HIGH for 8 to 11½ mintes, or until cheese melts and bubbles.

Makes 4 servings.

SPLIT PEA SOUP

4 cups hot water
1 12-ounce package dried split peas
½ pound bacon, diced
1 cup chopped onion
1 cup chopped celery
½ cup chopped carrot
¼ teaspoon pepper
¼ teaspoon ground thyme
small pinch ground cloves or allspice
1 to 1½ teaspoon salt

1. Combine all ingredients, except for salt, in a 2-quart glass casserole. Cover. Set microwave oven at power level HIGH for 15 minutes, and then power level LOW & DEFROST for 60 minutes. Stir occasionally.
2. Turn soup into blender or food processor and puree. Add salt to taste. If necessary, reheat the soup by microwaving, covered, at power level HIGH for 3 to 4 minutes. Add water if soup is too thick.

Makes 4 to 5 servings.

BOUILLABAISSE

1 small lobster tail
1 pound fish fillets
6 to 8 medium clams in shells

¾ cup chopped onion
1 clove garlic, pressed or finely chopped
⅛ cup oil, preferably olive oil
1 8-ounce can tomatoes, with their juice
½ cup water
⅛ cup chopped parsley
1 teaspoon dried basil
1 bay leaf
½ teaspoon salt
⅛ teaspoon pepper

1. Thaw fish if frozen. Split lobster tails in half lengthwise, then cut each length into quarters. Cut fish fillets into 1-inch chunks. Wash clams thoroughly. Set all fish aside.
2. Combine onion, garlic, and oil in a 2-quart glass casserole. Microwave, uncovered, at power level HIGH for 4 minutes, stirring once. Add remaining ingredients, except for fish, stirring briskly to break to break up to tomatoes. Cover. Microwave at power level HIGH for 10 minutes, stirring twice.
3. Add fish. Cover. Microwave at power level HIGH for 10 to 13 minutes, or until lobster and fish are cooked and clams open, stirring gently 3 times. Let stand 5 minutes before serving.

Makes 3 servings.

MANHATTAN CLAM CHOWDER

1 11-ounce can condensed vegetable soup
1½ cups tomato juice
1 7½-ounce can minced clams, with their juice
big pinch ground thyme
⅛ teaspoon pepper

1. Combine all ingredients in a 2-quart glass bowl.
2. Cover and microwave at power level HIGH for 10 to 13 minutes, or until hot, stirring 3 times. Serve with oyster crackers or saltiness

Makes 4 servings.

MEAT

Stuffed Flank Steak
(Recipe on page 27)

TIPS ON DEFROSTING MEAT

- Check package material to be sure there is no metal present.
- If package is completely nonmetallic, leave meat in original wrapping.
- Place package of meat in a shallow baking dish to catch juices.
- Meats weighing under 4 pounds should be defrosted at power level LOW & DEFROST. Meats weighing over 4 pounds should be started at power level HIGH and finished at power level LOW & DEFROST. Consult talble for power levels and times used in defrosting various meats.
- Separate pieces of meat during defrosting whenever possible.
- Meat is ready for standing time as soon as a fork can be pushed into the center of the meat using moderate pressure. The center of the meat will still be icy. Allow the meat to stand until completely thawed.

MEAT DEFROSTING TABLE

MEAT	AMOUNT	POWER LEVEL	DEFROSTING TIME	STANDING TIME
BEEF				
frankfurter	1 lb.	LOW & DEFROST	5-6 minutes	10 minutes
ground beef	1 lb.	LOW & DEFROST	8-10 minutes	10 minutes
kidney	2 lbs.	LOW & DEFROST	8-12 minutes	10 minutes
liver	1 lb.	LOW & DEFROST	6-7 minutes	10 minutes
roast, blade	3 lbs.	LOW & DEFROST	18-20 minutes	15 minutes
roast, chuck	3-4 lbs.	LOW & DEFROST	22-26 minutes	15 minutes
roast, rib (rolled)	3-4 lbs.	LOW & DEFROST	15-20 minutes	15 minutes
	7-8 lbs.	HIGH→LOW & DEFROST	9→20-25 minutes	20 minutes
roast, rump (boneless)	3-4 lbs.	LOW & DEFROST	20-25 minutes	15 minutes
	6-7 lbs.	HIGH→LOW & DEFROST	9→20-25 minutes	20 minutes
roast, sirloin tip	4-5 lbs.	HIGH→LOW & DEFROST	10→15-20 minutes	20 minutes
steak, cubed	1 lb.	LOW & DEFROST	7-8 minutes	10 minutes
steak, flank	1½ lbs.	LOW & DEFROST	9-10 minutes	10 minutes
steak, rib eye	2-3 lbs.	LOW & DEFROST	10-14 minutes	10 minutes
steak, round	2 lbs.	LOW & DEFROST	10-14 minutes	10 minutes
steak, sirloin	2 lbs.	LOW & DEFROST	10-12 minutes	10 minutes
VEAL				
chop	1 lb.	LOE & DEFROST	9-10 minutes	10 minutes
ground veal	1 lb.	LOW & DEFROST	4-5 minutes	10 minutes
steak	1 lb.	LOW & DEFROST	6-8 minutes	10 minutes
PORK				
bacon	1 lb.	LOW & DEFROST	4-6 minutes	10 minutes
chop (½" thick)	1½ lbs.	LOW & DEFROST	10-15 minutes	10 minutes
cubes	1½ lbs.	LOW & DEFROST	8-10 minutes	10 minutes
ground pork	1 lb.	LOW & DEFROST	5-6 minutes	10 minutes
roast, loin (boneless)	4-5 lbs.	HIGH→LOW & DEFROST	9→15-21 minutes	20 minutes
spareribs	3 lbs.	LOW & DEFROST	12-17 minutes	15 minutes
steak, shoulder	2½ lbs.	LOW & DEFROST	12-15 minutes	10 minutes
tenderloin	1 lbs.	LOW & DEFROST	10-12 minutes	10 minutes
LAMB				
roast, leg or shoulder	4-5 lbs.	HIGH→LOW & DEFROST	9→15-20 minutes	15 minutes
shanks	1 lb.	LOW & DEFROST	5-8 minutes	10 minutes
steak	2½ lbs.	LOW & DEFROST	12-15 minutes	10 minutes

TIPS ON COOKING MEAT

- Be sure meat is completely defrosted before proceeding to cook.
- Arrange meat so that thicker portions face the outside of the baking dish.
- Trim off excess fat.
- Drain juices as they accumulate in the baking dish. If desired, reserve juices for making gravy or sauce.
- Shield thin or bony portions of meats with strips of aluminum foil to prevent overcooking. Wooden toothpicks may be used to hold aluminum foil in place.
- Let meat stand, covered with aluminum foil, 10 to 15 minutes after it is removed from the microwave oven. During standing time, the internal temperature of the meat will rise as much as 15°F.

CONVENIENCE MEAT COOKING TABLE

CONVENIENCE MEAT	NUMBER	POWER LEVEL	COOKING TIME	STANDING TIME
bacon slices	2	HIGH	2-2½ minutes	—
	3		2½-4 minutes	—
	4		4-5 minutes	—
	8		6-9 minutes	—
Canadian bacon slices	2	HIGH	2-3 minutes	1 minute
	4		3-5 minutes	1 minute
	8		4½-6 minutes	1 minute
frankfurters	2	HIGH	2½-4 minutes	2 minutes
	4		4-5½ minutes	2 minutes
ham slices, 2 oz. each	2	HIGH	2-3 minutes	1 minute
	4		3-5 minutes	1 minute
hamburgers, fresh 4 oz. each	1	HIGH	1½-2 minutes	2 minutes
	2		2-3½ minutes	2 minutes
	4		3½-5½ minutes	3 minutes
hamburgers, frozen 3½ oz. each	1	HIGH	3-3½ minutes	3 minutes
	2		4-5 minutes	3 minutes
	4		6-7 minutes	3 minutes
sausage links, fresh, 1-2 oz. each	2	HIGH	2½-4 minutes	2 minutes
	4		5-7½ minutes	2 minutes
	8		4½-11 minutes	2 minutes
sausage links, brown-and-serve, frozen.	2	HIGH	1-2½ minutes	2 minutes
	4		2½ minutes	2 minutes
	8		2½ minutes	2 minutes
sausage patties, fresh, 1-2 oz. each	2	HIGH	2½-4 minutes	2 minutes
	4		5-7½ minutes	2 minutes

BEEF & VEAL

STUFFED FLANK STEAK

1 cup finely chopped onion
1 clove garlic, pressed or finely chopped
4 tablespoons butter or margarine
1 10-ounce package frozen chopped
    spinach, thawed and well drained
⅛ teaspoon ground thyme
¼ teaspoon salt
¼ teaspoon pepper

1 beef flank steak, about 1½ pounds
    cut in half
1 cup strong beef broth
1 11-ounce can condensed cream of
    mushroom soup
¼ cup white wine (optional)

1. Combine onion, garlic, and butter in a 1½-quart glass bowl. Microwave, uncovered, at power level HIGH for 6 to 7½ minutes, or until onion is soft, stirring once. Stir in spinach, thyme, salt, and pepper. Cover Microwave at power level HIGH for 4 minutes, stirring once.
2. Pound flank steak with mallet to flatten. Spread spinach mixture on steak and roll up like a jelly roll. Tie with string or skewer with wooden picks cut in half. Place in a 2-quart glass casserole.
3. Combine remaining ingredients and pour over steak. Cover. Set microwave oven at power level HIGH for 15 minutes. Turn steaks over, cover and then microwave at power level LOW & DEFROST for 25½ minutes or until tender. Let stand, covered, for 10 minutes before serving.

Makes 4 servings.

CUBED STEAKS WITH MUSHROOM SAUCE

1 tablespoon cornstarch
1 tablespoon instant beef bouillon
¼ cup dry white or red wine
2 4-ounce cans sliced mushrooms, with
    their juice
1 teaspoon Worcestershire sauce
½ teaspoon salt
¼ teaspoon pepper

4 large beef cubed steaks (4 ounces or more
    each)

1. Combine cornstarch and instant beef bouillon in a small bowl. Gradually add the wine, stirring to make a smooth paste. Stir in the remaining ingredients, except steaks.
2. Lay steaks in a 2-quart glass casserole. Pour mushroom mixture over them. Cover. Microwave at power level HIGH for 10 to 13 minutes, or until steaks are done. Let stand, covered, 5 minutes before serving.

Makes 4 servings.

OLD-FASHIONED BEEF STEW

2 pounds beef stew meat
2 tablespoons oil or bacon drippings

¼ cup flour
1 16-ounce can tomatoes
½ cup beef broth
½ cup cold coffee
2 medium potatoes, peeled and cubed
2 medium carrots, scraped and sliced
2 medium onions, sliced
2 ribs celery, sliced
1 tablespoon tomato paste
½ teaspoon whole thyme leaves
½ teaspoon salt
¼ teaspoon pepper

1. Combine meat and oil in a 3-quart glass casserole Cover. Microwave at power level HIGH for 10 minutes, stirring once.
2. Stir flour into meat. Add remaining ingredients. Cover. Set microwave oven at power level HIGH for 10 minutes, and then power level LOW & DEFROST for 76 minutes. Stir after 30 minutes' cooking time. If meat is not fork-tender, microwave at power level LOW & DEFROST an additional 19 minutes.

Makes 6 servings.

HUNGARIAN GOULASH

¼ cup oil or bacon drippings
1½ cups chopped onion
2 pounds beef stew meat

2 tablespoons flour
1 cup beef broth
1 cup tomato juice
1 tablespoon paprika
½ teaspoon salt
¼ to ½ teaspoon pepper

1. Combine oil, onion, and stew meat in a 3-quart glass casserole. Cover. Microwave at power level HIGH for 10 minutes, stirring once.
2. Stir flour into onion-beef mixture. Add remaining ingredients. Set microwave oven at power level HIGH for 9 minutes, and then power level LOW & DEFROST for 76 minutes. Stir twice. If beef is not forktender, microwave at power level LOW & DEFROST additional 19 mintes. Serve over noodles.

Makes 6 servings.

BEEF STROGANOFF

3 tablespoons butter or margarine
½ cup chopped onion

1 pound boneless steak, cut into thin strips
1 cup sliced fresh mushrooms
big pinch whole thyme leaves
½ teaspoon salt
¼ teaspoon pepper

beef broth
3 to 4 tablespoons flour
½ to 1 cup sour cream or yoghurt

1. Combine butter and onion in a 10-inch round baking dish. Microwave, uncovered, at power level HIGH for 4 to 5 minutes, or until onion is fairly soft, stirring once.
2. Add beef, mushrooms, and seasonings. Microwave, uncovered, at power level HIGH for 10 to 12 minutes, or until beef is tender, stirring twice.
3. Drain liquid from beef into a 2-cup measure. Add enough beef broth to measure to equal ¾ cup. Set aside. Stir flour into meat, blending until smooth. Slowly add juice and broth mixture. Stir. Microwave, uncovered, at power level HIGH for 2 to 3 minutes, or until sauce is thickened, stirring once. Stir in sour cream or yoghurt. Microwave at power level LOW & DEFROST for 4 to 5 minutes, stirring every minute. Do not let sauce boil or sour cream will curdle.

Makes 3 to 4 servings.

ITALIAN PEPPER STEAK

¼ cup oil
3 medium green peppers, cut into thin strips
3 medium onions, thinly sliced
1 pound boneless steak, cut into thin strips
¾ teaspoon salt
¼ teaspoon pepper

1. Combine oil, green peppers, and onions in a 10-inch round baking dish. Microwave, uncovered, at power level HIGH for 9 to 11½ minutes, or until vegetables are soft, stirring twice.
2. Add steak and seasonings. Microwave, uncovered, at power level HIGH for 8 to 9 minutes, or until beef is cooked, stirring twice. Serve over rice or in hero rolls.

Makes 3 to 4 servings.

CHEESY MEATLOAF

1½ pounds ground beef
1 egg
1½ cups soft, fresh bread crumbs
1 8-ounce can tomato sauce
1 cup shredded American cheese
½ cup finely chopped onion
¼ cup finely chopped green pepper
½ teaspoon whole thyme leaves, crushed
½ teaspoon salt
¼ teaspoon pepper

1. Combine all ingredients in a medium mixing bowl. Blend thoroughly.
2. Spread mixture evenly in a glass loaf dish. Cover with wax paper. Microwave at power level HIGH for 18 to 22½ minutes, or until center is no longer pink. Let stand, covered, 5 minutes before serving.

Makes 6 servings.

ITALIAN MEATBALLS

½ pound ground beef
1 egg
¼ cup cracker crumbs
¼ cup grated Parmesan cheese
1 clove garlic, pressed or finely chopped
½ tablespoon dried parsley flakes
½ teaspoon oregano leaves
⅛ teaspoon whole thyme leaves
¼ teaspoon salt
⅛ teaspoon pepper

1 8-ounce can tomatoes, chopped
½ cup greated Parmesan cheese

1. Combine all ingredients, except canned tomatoes and last ½ cup grated Parmesan cheese, in medium mixing bowl. Shape into 12 1¼-inch meatballs. Arrange meatballs in a 10-inch round baking dish. Microwave, uncovered, at power level HIGH for 3 to 4 minutes, or until meatballs are nearly done, rearranging the meatballs once.
2. Pour chopped tomatoes over meatballs and sprinkle with ½ cup grated Parmesan cheese. Cover. Microwave at power level HIGH for about 3 minutes, or until heated through.

Makes 2 to 3 servings.

TACOS

1 pound lean ground beef
¼ cup finely minced green pepper
3 cloves garlic, pressed or finely chopped
1 tablespoon tomato paste
1½ to 2 teaspoons chili powder
¼ teaspoon ground thyme
½ teaspoon salt

12 taco shells
1½ cups shredded Cheddar cheese
1 cup finely chopped onion
3 cups shredded lettuce

1. Combine ground beef and green pepper in a 1½-quart glass casserole. Cover. Microwave at power level HIGH for 6 minutes, stirring once. Stir in tomato paste and seasonings. Cover. Microwave at power level HIGH for 6 to 9 minutes, or until mixture bubbles, stirring once. Let stand, covered, 5 minutes.
2. Divide beef mixture between taco shells. Top first with grated cheese, then with tomato, onion, and lettuce.

Makes 4 to 6 servings.

BEEF LIVER WITH ONIONY CREAM SAUCE

6 slices bacon
1 pound beef liver, thinly sliced
1 11-ounce can condensed cream of mushroom soup
1 envelope dehydrated onion soup mix
¼ cup water

1. Arrange bacon in a 10-inch round baking dish and cover with wax paper. Microwave at power level HIGH for 6 minutes, or until bacon is crisp. Remove bacon from dish, crumble, and set aside.
2. Arrange liver in baking dish, turning once to coat both sides with bacon drippings. Microwave, uncovered, at power level HIGH for 2½ minutes. Turn liver over.
3. Blend remaining ingredients together in a small bowl. Pour over liver. Cover. Set microwave oven at power level HIGH for 6 minutes, and then power level LOW & DEFROST for 9½ minutes. If liver is not done to taste, microwave at power level LOW & DEFROST an additional 4½ to 8 minutes. Top with reserved bacon. Serve over rice.

Makes 4 servings.

SWEET AND SOUR CABBAGE ROLLS

8 large cabbage leaves

1 pound ground beef
½ cup cooked rice
½ cup finely chopped onion
½ cup ketchup
½ cup raisins
1 teaspoon salt
¼ teaspoon pepper

1 8-ounce can tomato sauce
½ cup ginger snap crumbs
⅓ cup cider vinegar

1. Place cabbage leaves in a 2½-quart glass casserole. Cover. Microwave at power level HIGH for 4 to 6 minutes, or until leaves are soft enough to fold easily. Set aside.
2. Combine beef, rice, onion, ketchup, raisins, salt, and pepper in a medium mixing bowl. Mix well. Stuff cabbage leaves with this filling, rolling up cigar fashion and folding in the edges. Place stuffed cabbage leaves seam-side-down in a glass casserole.
3. Combine remaining ingredients in a small bowl. Pour over stuffed cabbage leaves. Cover. Microwave at power level HIGH for 11½ to 13½ minutes, or until cabbage rolls feel firm when pressed with the back of a spoon. Let stand, covered, 5 minutes before serving.

Makes 4 servings.

VEAL PAPRIKA

1 pound boneless veal, cut into 1½-inch cubes
2 cups sliced fresh mushrooms
1 cup chicken broth
½ cup finely chopped onion
1 tablespoon paprika
¼ teaspoon ground thyme
½ teaspoon salt
¼ teaspoon pepper

¼ cup dry white wine or dry sherry
3 tablespoons flour
½ to 1 cup sour cream

1. Combine veal, mushrooms, chicken broth, onion, and seasonings in a 3-quart glass casserole. Cover. Set microwave oven at power level HIGH for 6 minutes, and then power level LOW & DEFROST for 32 minutes. Stir twice. If veal is not fork-tender, microwave at power level LOW & DEFROST an additional 13 minutes.
2. Blend wine and flour together until smooth. Stir into veal. Cover. Microwave at power level HIGH for 2½ to 4 minutes, or until sauce is thickened. Stir in the sour cream. Reheat, if necessary, by microwaving at power level LOW & DEFROST for 2½ to 4 minutes, stirring every minute. Do not allow to boil or sour cream will curdle.

Makes 4 servings.

VEAL RUMP ROAST

2½-pound bone-in veal rump roast
½ cup white wine
1 tablespoon dried parsley flakes
¼ teaspoon whole thyme leaves
½ teaspoon salt
¼ teaspoon pepper
1 medium onion, sliced
1 rib celery, sliced
1 medium carrot, scraped and sliced
1 small bay leaf

¼ cup chicken broth or white wine
2 to 3 tablespoons flour

1. Place veal roast fat-side-down in a 3-quart glass casserole. Pour wine over roast. Sprinkle meat with parsley, thyme, salt, and pepper. Sprinkle vegetables and bay leaf over and around roast.
2. Cover and microwave at power level HIGH for 15 minutes. Turn roast fat-side-up. Cover. Microwave at power level LOW & DEFROST for 40 to 50 minutes, or until fork-tender. Let stand, covered, while you prepare the gravy.
3. Pour pan juices into a 4-cup glass measure through a strainer. For every half cup of liquid, stir 1 tablespoon flour into the ¼ cup wine. Blend flour and wine to a smooth paste, then beat paste into pan juices. Microwave at power level HIGH for 4 to 5 minutes, or until gravy is bubbly and thickened, stirring once.

Makes 4 to 6 servings.

PORK & LAMB

APPLE-STUFFED PORK CHOPS

4 center-cut pork chops, ¾-inch thick
   (1½ to 2 pounds)
¼ teaspoon pepper
½ cup finely chopped apple
¼ cup finely chopped celery
3 tablespoons raisins
1 tablespoon finely chopped green onion
¼ teaspoon rubbed sage
⅛ teaspoon ground cinnamon
¼ cup apple juice
3 to 3½ teaspoons instand beef bouillon

½ cup apple juice
2 tablespoons flour
½ teaspoon salt

1. Cut pocket in each chop and rub with pepper. In a small bowl, combine apple, celery, raisins, green onion, sage, and cinnamon. Use this mixture to stuff pork chops. Secure opening with toothpicks or wooden skewers. Arrange chops in a 2-quart glass casserole. Pour ¼ cup apple juice over chops, then sprinkle chops with instant beef bouillion. Cover. Microwave at power level LOW & DEFROST for 27 to 32 minutes, or until chops are tender. Let stand, covered, 5 minutes.
2. Blend remaining ½ cup apple juice and flour together in a 4-cup measure. Add salt. Pour pan juices from pork chops into measure and blend well. Microwave at power level HIGH for 4 to 5 minutes, or until hot and thickened, stirring once. Serve this gravy with pork chops.

Makes 4 servings.

CURRIED PORK CHOPS

1 11-ounce can cream of mushroom soup
1 medium apple, peeled, cored, and finely
   chopped
½ cup finely chopped onion
½ cup raisins
¼ cup whipping cream
2 to 3 teaspoons curry powder
¼ teaspoon ground thyme
¼ teaspoon salt
¼ teaspoon pepper

4 pork chops, ¾ inch thick (1½ to 2
   pounds)

1. Combine all ingredients, except pork chops, in mixing bowl and blend well.
2. Arrange pork chops in a 2-quart glass casserole. Pour curry mixture on top. Cover. Microwave at power level LOW & DEFROST for 24 to 32 minutes, or until chops are tender. Let stand, covered, 5 minutes before serving.

Makes 4 servings.

PORK CHOPS WITH CANDIED YAMS

4 to 6 pork chops (about 1¼ pounds)
¼ teaspoon salt
¼ teaspoon pepper

2 16-to 18-ounce cans candied sweet
   potatoes or yams
¼ teaspoon rubbed sage
pinch ground cinnamon
pinch groun nutmeg
1 large orange, thinly sliced, seeds removed

2 tablespoons orange juice
½ tablespoon cornstarch

1. Arrange pork chops in a 10-inch round baking dish. Sprinkle with salt and pepper. Cover. Microwave at power level HIGH for 15 minutes.
2. Slice the sweet potatoes thickly and arrange on top of the pork chops. Sprinkle with sage, cinnamon, and nutmeg. Top evenly with orange slices. Cover. Microwave at power level HIGH for 10 to 12 minutes, or until chops are tender. Remove chops and sweet potatoes to a serving platter and cover.
3. Blend orange juice and cornstarch. Add cornstarch mixture to the pan juices. Blending well. Microwave, uncovered, at power level HIGH for 2½ to 4 minutes, or until sauce is bubbly and thickened. Spoon over chops.

Makes 3 servings.

Tacos
(Recipe on page 29)

SMOKED PORK CHOPS WITH BAKED BEANS

4 slices bacon

½ cup finely chopped onion
2 14-ounce cans pork and beans in
    molasses sauce
1 tablespoon Worcestershire sauce
3 to 4 drops liquid smoke
4 smoked pork chops, about 1 pound

1. Place bacon in a 2-quart glass casserole. Cover with wax paper. Microwave at power level HIGH for 4½ minutes, or until crisp. Crumble and set aside.
2. Add onion to bacon drippings in baking dish. Microwave, uncovered, at power level HIGH for 5 minutes, stirring once. Stir in beans, Worcestershire sauce, and liquid smoke. Add the pork chops, spooning the bean mixture over them.
3. Cover with wax paper. Microwave at power level HIGH for 11½ minutes, or until hot. Let stand, covered, 2 to 3 minutes before serving. Top with crumbled bacon.

Makes 4 servings

SOUTH SEAS PORK CHOPS

1 pound boneless pork, cut into 1-inch
    cubes
1 large onion, thinly sliced

1 16-ounce can pineapple chunks, drained
2 cups fresh broccoli flowerets
1 cup slivered almonds
1 2-ounce jar sliced pimento
2 tablespoons cornstarch
2 tablespoons packed dark brown sugar
2 tablespoons soy sauce
2 tablespoons sherry or pineapple juice
1 teaspoon ground ginger
1 teaspoon salt

1. Combine pork and onion in a 3-quart glass casserole. Cover. Microwave at power level HIGH for 9 minutes, stirring once.
2. Add all remaining ingredients, stirring well to blend. Cover. Microwave at power level HIGH for 9 to 11½ minutes, or until pork is tender, stirring twice. Let stand, covered, 5 minutes before serving. Serve over rice, if desired.

Makes 4 servings.

BARBECUED RIBS

¾ cup ketchup
¾ cup orange or apple juice
3 tablespoons cider vinegar
3 tablespoons finely chopped onion
1½ tablespoons packed dark brown sugar
2 cloves garlic, pressed or finely
    chopped
¼ teaspoon hot pepper sauce
¾ teaspoon salt

2½ pounds pork loin back ribs

1. Combine all ingredients, except ribs, in a 1-quart glass bowl. Microwave, uncovered, at power level HIGH for 9 minutes, stirring twice. Set aside.
2. Cut ribs into 3 to 4 serving pieces. Arrange in a 10-inch round baking dish, overlapping slightly. Cover and microwave at power level HIGH for 11 minutes. Rearrange ribs, recover and microwave at power level HIGH for 8½ minutes. Drain off juices and rearrange ribs in dish once again. Pour barbecue sauce over ribs.
3. Microwave, uncovered, at power level HIGH for 15 minutes. Rearrange ribs and baste with sauce. Microwave uncovered at power level HIGH for 3 to 7½ minutes or until ribs are tender.

Makes 4 to 6 servings.

TROPICAL HAM KABOBS

1 tablespoon butter or margarine
1 tablespoon lemon juice
1 tablespoon packed dark brown sugar
1 tablespoon honey
1 teaspoon soy sauce
½ teaspoon ground ginger
pinch ground cloves

¾ pound cooked ham, cut into 1-inch cubes
1 16-ounce can pineapple chunks
2 medium bananas, cut into 1-inch slices

1. Combine butter, lemon juice, brown sugar, honey, soy sauce, ginger, and cloves in a 2-cup glass measure. Microwave at power level HIGH for 1 to 1½ minutes, or until butter is melted, stirring twice.
2. Thread ham, pineapple, and banana alternately on six 8-inch skewers. (Use wooden skewers if possible, though metal ones may also be used.) Arrange kabobs in a 10-inch round baking dish. Brush with the butter sauce. Microwave at power level HIGH for 7½ minutes, or until heated through, turning the skewers and basting with remaining butter sauce after 3 minutes.

Makes 4 servings.

FRANKS IN BEER

1 pound frankfurters
1 12-ounce can beer, at room temperature
½ cup finely chopped onion

1. Arrange frankfurters in a 2-quart glass casserole. Pour beer over frankfurters. Sprinkle on onions.
2. Cover. Microwave at power level HIGH for 7 to 9 minutes, or until heated. Let stand, covered, 5 minutes before serving.

Makes 4 to 5 servings.

RING BOLOGNA AND SAUERKRAUT

1 27-ounce can sauerkraut
1 medium carrot, shredded
1 small onion, finely chopped
2 teaspoons dried parsley flakes
1 to 2 teaspoons caraway seeds
¼ teaspoon pepper
1 precooked ring bologna, 1 to 1½ pounds

1. In a 2-quart glass bowl, mix all ingredients together, except for bologna. Place bologna on top.
2. Cover. Microwave at power level HIGH for 10 to 13½ minutes, or until hot. Let stand, covered, 5 minutes before serving.

Makes 4 servings.

KIELBASA SAUSAGE WITH RED CABBAGE

1 1-pound head red cabbage, shredded
1 medium tart apple, peeled and shredded
⅛ cup packed light brown sugar
⅛ cup cider vinegar
⅛ cup finely chopped onion
½ teaspoon grated lemon peel
¼ teaspoon caraway seeds
¼ teaspoon salt
⅛ teaspoon pepper
1 Kielbasa sausage, about 1 pound

1. Combine all ingredients, except sausage, in a 2-quart glass casserole. Cover. Microwave at power level HIGH for 7 to 10 minutes, stirring twice.
2. Pierce Kielbasa thoroughly and arrange on top of cabbage. Cover. Microwave at power level HIGH for 10 to 14 minutes, or until heated through. Let stand, covered, for 5 minutes before serving.

Makes 3 to 4 servings.

DEVILED LAMB CHOPS

¼ cup prepared mustard
¼ cup finely chopped green onion
2 tablespoons oil, preferably olive oil
2 cloves garlic, pressed or finely chopped
2 tablespoons dried parsley flakes
¼ teaspoon salt
¼ teaspoon ground thyme
⅛ teaspoon pepper
4 shoulder lamb chops, about 1 pound

1 Combine all ingredients, except lamb chops, in a small bowl. Arrange chops in a 2-quart glass casserole. Paint with half of the mustard mixture.
2. Cover. Microwave at power level LOW & DEFROST for 8 minutes. Turn chops over and paint with remaining mustard mixture. Cover. Microwave at power level LOW & DEFROST for 4½ to 9½ minutes longer, or until chops are done to taste.
Let stand, covered, 5 minutes before serving.

Makes 2 to 4 servings.

MEXICAN-STYLE LAMB CHOPS

1 8-ounce can tomato sauce
¼ cup finely chopped onion
¼ cup finely chopped green pepper
¼ cup finely chopped celery
1 clove garlic, pressed or finely chopped
½ to 1 teaspoon chili powder
½ teaspoon salt
¼ to ½ teaspoon pepper
4 shoulder lamb chops, about 1 pound

1. Combine all ingredients, except lamb chops, in a 2-quart glass casserole. Cover. Microwave at power level HIGH for 6 minutes, stirring once.
2. Place lamb chops in baking dish with sauce. Spoon sauce over top of chops. Cover. Microwave at power level LOW & DEFROST for 12½ to 16 minutes. Let stand, covered, 5 minutes before serving.

Makes 2 to 4 servings.

SPICY LAMB KABOBS

½ cup lemon juice
¼ cup oil, preferably olive oil
3 cloves garlic, pressed or finely chopped
2 teaspoons curry powder
2 bay leaves
½ teaspoon salt
1 pound boneless lamb, cur into 1½-inch chunks
8 small onions, peeled
12 cherry tomatoes
1 large sweet potato, cut into 1-inch chunks
2 green peppers

1. Combine lemon juice, oil, garlic, curry powder, bay leaves, and salt in a 2-quart glass or ceramic mixing bowl. Add lamb and stir to coat with marinade. Cover and allow lamb to marinate in the refrigerator for 3 hours or more, stirring occasionally.
2. Remove lamb from bowl, reserving marinade. Thread lamb, onion, cherry tomatoes, sweet potato, and green pepper alternately on six 8-inch skewers. (Use wooden skewers if possible, though metal ones may also be used.) Brush liberally with reserved marinade. Arrange kabobs on a 10-inch round baking dish, with the skewers overlapping the edges of the dish at each end. Microwave at power level HIGH for 8 to 10 minutes, rearranging the kabobs and basting with marinade after 4 minutes. Cover and let stand 5 minutes before serving.

Makes 4 servings.

Orange Glazed Duck
(Recipe on page 47)

POULTRY DEFROSTING
TABLE***

POULTRY	AMOUT	POWER LEVEL	DEFROSTING TIME	STANDING TIME
CHICKEN				
whole	3-4 lbs.		24-28 minutes	20 minutes
parts	2½-3 lbs.		12-15 minutes	15 minutes
breasts (bone-in)	2-3 lbs.	LOW & DEFROST	8-12 minutes	20 minutes
drumsticks	1 lb.		7-8 minutes	10 minutes
thighs	1 lb.		7-8 minutes	10 minutes
wings	1½ lbs.		6-10 minutes	10 minutes
CAPON, WHOLE	6-8 lbs.	HIGH→LOW & DEFROST	9→15-25 minutes	30 minutes
CORNISH HENS, WHOLE	3½-4 lbs.	LOW & DEFROST	22-28 minutes	25 minutes
TURKEY				
whole	8 lbs.	HIGH→LOW & DEFROST	13½→15-25 minutes	30 minutes
parts	2-3 lbs.	LOW & DEFROST	12-15 minutes	15 minutes
breast (bone-in)	4-5 lbs.	HIGH→LOW & DEFROST	4½→10-15 minutes	20 minutes
DUCKLING, WHOLE	4-5 lbs.	HIGH→LOW & DEFROST	9→15-25 minutes	25 minutes
GOOSE, WHOLE	8 lbs.	HIGH→LOW & DEFROST	13½→15-25 minutes	25 minutes
PHEASANT, WHOLE	2-3 lbs.	LOW & DEFROST	12-15 minutes	20 minutes

***Before proceeding to defrost poultry in your microwave oven, please read through "TIPS ON DEFROSTING MEAT" on page 22.

TIPS ON COOKING POULTRY

- Be sure poultry is completely defrosted before proceeding to cook.
- Arrange poultry so that thicker, meatier pieces face the outside of the baking dish.
- Since poultry has a tendency to splatter and pop as it heats, it is a good idea to cover the baking dish with wax paper or parchment paper.
- Be sure that stuffing is hot when it is placed inside whole poultry. Cold stuffing will slow cooking time.
- Drain juices as they accumulate in the baking dish. If you wish, reserve the juices and use them to make sauce or gravy.
- Shield any thin or bony pieces of poultry with strips of aluminum foil to prevent overcooking. Wooden toothpicks may be used to hold aluminum foil in place.
- Standing time is essential to complete the cooking process. Avoid overcooking poultry in your microwave oven, or white meat will become dry and stringy.

POULTRY COOKING TABLE

POULTRY	AMOUNT	POWER LEVEL	COOKING TIME	STANDING TIME
CHICKEN				
whole	3-4 lbs.	HIGH	32-45 minutes	10 minutes
half	1-1½ lbs.	HIGH	13-15 minutes	10 minutes
parts	2½-3 lbs.	HIGH	20-23 minutes	10 minutes
breasts (bone-in)	2½-3 lbs.	HIGH	18-20 minutes	10 minutes
drumsticks	2½-3 lbs.	HIGH	20-23 minutes	10 minutes
CAPON, WHOLE	6-8 lbs.	HIGH	75-90 minutes	15 minutes
CORNISH HENS, WHOLE	3½-4 lbs.	HIGH	25-30 minutes	10 minutes
TURKEY				
whole	8 lbs.	HIGH	60-80 minutes	15 minutes
parts	2-3 lbs.	HIGH	40-45 minutes	10 minutes
breast (bone-in)	4-5 lbs.	HIGH	50-65 minutes	10 minutes
DUCKLING, WHOLE	4-5 lbs.	LOW & DEFROST	85-100 minutes	10 minutes
GOOSE, WHOLE	8 lbs.	LOW & DEFROST	110-120 minutes	15 minutes
PHEASANT, WHOLE	2-3 lbs.	HIGH	18-22 minutes	10 minutes

CONVENIENCE POULTRY COOKING TABLE

CONVENIENCE POULTRY	AMOUNT	POWER LEVEL	COOKING TIME
barbecued chicken, frozen	5-to 6½-ounce pouch*	HIGH	4-6 minutes
chicken a la king, frozen	12-ounce pouch*	HIGH	9-13 minutes
chicken croquettes, thawed	12-ounce package	HIGH	5-7 minutes
fried chicken, precooked and thawed	2 medium pieces	HIGH	3-6 minutes
sliced turkey with gravy, frozen	12-ounce pouch*	HIGH	10-14 minutes
turkey tetrazzini, frozen	5-to 6½-ounce pouch*	HIGH	4-6 minutes

* *Slit pouch and place in a baking dish before placing in microwave oven.*

ROAST CHICKEN WITH CORN BREAD STUFFING

½ cup thinly sliced celery
½ cup chopped onion
4 tablespoons butter or margarine

1 12-ounce package corn bread mix, baked
   and crumbled
1 egg
¾ cup chicken broth
½ to 1 teaspoon rubbed sage or poultry
   seasoning
½ teaspoon salt
¼ teaspoon pepper
5 to 5½-pound whole roasting chicken
2 tablespoons instant beef broth dissolved
   in 4 tablespoons water

1. Combine celery, onion, and butter in a 2-quart glass bowl. Microwave, uncovered, at power level HIGH for 6 to 9 minutes, or until vegetables are very tender, stirring twice.
2. Add all remaining ingredients, except for chicken and beef broth. Blend thoroughly. Cover. Microwave at power level LOW & DEFROST for 5 to 6 minutes, or until hot, stirring once.
3. Stuff chicken with hot stuffing. Sew vent shut. Tie legs and wings to the body. Arrange chicken on a microwave-safe roasting rack set in a baking dish. Brush, if desired, with dissolved beef broth. Microwave, uncovered, at power level HIGH for 70 to 80 minutes, or until meat near the bone is no longer pink. Let stand, covered with foil, for 10 minutes before serving.

Makes 6 to 8 servings.

BARBECUED CHICKEN

2½ to 3 pounds chicken, cut into serving
   pieces
1 cup barbecue sauce

1. Arrange chicken in a 10-inch round baking dish, with the meatier, thicker portions facing toward the edge of the dish. Cover with wax paper. Microwave at power level HIGH for 5 minutes. Drain and turn over.
2. Brush half of the barbecue sauce onto the chicken. Microwave, uncovered, at power level HIGH for 6 minutes. Turn, brush with remaining sauce, and continue to microwave at power level HIGH for an additional 5 to 9 minutes, or until chicken is tender. Let stand, covered, 5 minutes before serving.

Makes 4 servings.

CHICKEN CACCIATORE

1 15-ounce can tomatoes, broken up
1 4½-ounce can mushrooms, with their
   juice
2 tablespoons flour
3 cloves garlic, pressed or finely chopped
1 teaspoon dried basil or oregano
½ teaspoon whole thyme leaves
½ teaspoon salt
¼ teaspoon pepper
2½ to 3 pounds chicken, cut into serving
   pieces

1. Place tomatoes and mushrooms in a 10-inch round baking dish. Push solids to one side with a fork and stir flour into juices, blending until smooth. Add remaining ingredients and stir to blend together. Arrange the chicken in the dish, with the meatier, thicker parts facing outward. Spoon tomato mixture over chicken.
2. Cover dish with wax paper. Microwave at power level HIGH for 25 to 32 minutes, rearranging and turning over the chicken midway through the cooking period.
Let stand, covered, 5 minutes before serving.

Makes 4 servings.

COQ AU VIN

5 slices bacon, cut up
¼ cup flour
1 11-ounce can condensed beef broth
1 cup dry red wine
1 tablespoon tomato paste
¼ cup chopped green onion
1 to 2 cloves garlic, pressed or finely
   chopped
1 tablespoon dried parsley flakes
½ teaspoon whole thyme leaves
1 small bay leaf
½ teaspoon salt
¼ teaspoon pepper
2½ to 3 pounds chicken, cut into serving
   pieces
2 medium carrots, scraped and sliced

2 cups sliced fresh mushrooms

1. Place bacon in a 3-quart glass casserole. Cover with wax paper. Microwave at power level HIGH for 5 to 6 minutes, or until crisp. Blend flour into drippings. Stir in beef broth and wine. Add all remaining ingredients, except mushrooms.
2. Cover and microwave at power level HIGH for 15 minutes. Add mushrooms. Cover and microwave at power level HIGH for 9 minutes, or until chicken is cooked through, stirring once. Let stand, covered, 5 minutes before serving.

Makes 4 servings.

CHICKEN STEW WITH DUMPLINGS

2½ to 3 pounds chicken, cut into serving
   pieces
1 tablespoon dried parsley flakes
1 teaspoon paprika
½ teaspoon salt
¼ teaspoon pepper

1 11-ounce can condensed cream of
   chicken soup
⅔ cup milk or half-and-half

2 cups buttermilk baking mix
⅔ cup milk

1. Arrange chicken in a 10-inch round baking dish, with meatier, thicker portions facing toward the outer edge of the dish. Sprinkle with parsley flakes, paprika, salt, and pepper. Cover with wax paper. Microwave at power level HIGH for 19 minutes. Drain off juices.
2. Combine soup and milk. Pour over chicken. Cover and microwave at power level HIGH for 6 minutes, stirring once.
3. Mix baking mix and milk together in a small bowl to form a soft dough. Drop dumplings all around the edge of the dish. Microwave, uncovered, at power level HIGH for 9 to 10 minutes, or until dumplings are risen and light.

Makes 4 to 5 servings

CHICKEN PARMIGIANA

2 chicken breasts, boned, skinned, split
   lengthwise, and lightly pounded
   (1 to 1¼ pounds)
⅔ cup dry bread crumbs
⅓ cup grated Parmesan cheese
½ teaspoon dried basil
½ teaspoon salt
¼ teaspoon pepper
1 egg beaten with 2 teaspoons oil
2 tablespoons oil, preferably olive oil

1 8-ounce can tomato sauce
½ teaspoon dried basil.
1 cup shredded mozzarella cheese

1. Mix bread crumbs, Parmesan cheese, basil, salt, and pepper on a dinner plate. Dip the chicken pieces first in the crumb mixture, then in the beaten egg, then in the crumb mixture again. Use one tablespoon of the oil to coat the bottom of a 10-inch round baking dish. Arrange the chicken in the dish and drizzle with the remaining tablespoon oil. Microwave, uncovered, at power level HIGH for 5 to 7½ minutes.
2. Pour tomato sauce over chicken and sprinkle with remaining ½ teaspoon basil. Microwave at power level HIGH for 4 to 5 minutes, or until sauce is hot. Sprinkle on the mozzarella cheese. Let chicken stand, covered, for 5 minutes, or until cheese melts.

Makes 2 to 4 servings.

CHICKEN BREASTS WITH SNOW PEAS

6 chicken breasts, halved lengthwise (about 3 pounds)
2 tablespoons butter or margarine, melted
1 tablespoon soy sauce
1 tablespoon lemon juice
½ teaspoon salt
¼ teaspoon pepper

1 6-ounce package frozen snow peas, thawed
1 2½-ounce jar mushrooms, drained

1. Arrange chicken breasts in a 10-inch round baking dish, with meatier, thicker portions facing the outside edge of the dish. Combine all remaining ingredients, except snow peas and mushrooms, in a small bowl and brush this mixture over chicken. Cover with wax paper. Microwave at power level HIGH for 13 minutes.
2. Top chicken with snow peas and mushrooms. Cover and microwave at power level HIGH for 6 to 9 minutes, or until vegetables are heated through and chicken is fully cooked. Let stand, covered, 5 minutes before serving.

Makes 6 servings.

CHICKEN SALTIMBOCCA

2 chicken breasts, boned, skinned, and halved lengthwise (1 to 1¼ pounds)
4 slices boiled ham
2 large slices Swiss cheese, halved
¼ cup thick tomato sauce
½ teaspoon ground thyme

4 tablespoons butter or margarine
½ cup fine, dry bread crumbs
2 tablespoons grated Parmesan cheese
2 tablespoons finely chopped parsley

1. Place chicken between sheets of wax paper or plastic wrap and gently pound until each breast half enlarges to a rectangle approximately 6 × 5 inches. Discard wrap. Place a ham slice and half a cheese slice on each breast half. Spoon 1 tablespoon tomato sauce on top and sprinkle on a bit of thyme. Roll up the breasts like jelly rolls and fold in the sides.
2. Melt butter in a 10-inch round baking dish. Combine crumbs, cheese, and parsley on a plate. Dip chicken rolls first in butter, then in the cromb mixture. Arrange rolls seam-side-down in the baking dish. Cover with wax paper. Microwave at power level HIGH for 9 to 13 minutes. Let stand, covered, 5 minutes before serving. Serve with the pan juices.

Makes 2 to 4 servings.

CHICKEN ROULADES

1 cup chopped mushrooms
½ cup finely chopped onion
¼ cup finely chopped celery
1 clove garlic, pressed or finely chopped
3 tablespoons butter or margarine

2 tablespoons fine bread crumbs
1 tablespoon finely chopped parsley
¼ to teaspoon ground thyme
¼ to ½ teaspoon salt
¼ teaspoon pepper

2 chicken breasts, boned, skinned, and pounded to ¼-inch thickness (1 to 1¼ pounds)
1 11-ounce can cream of mushroom soup
¼ cup dry white wine or dry vermouth

1. Combine mushrooms, onion, celery, garlic, and butter in a 1-quart glass bowl. Microwave, uncovered, at power level HIGH for 5½ to 7 minutes, or until vegetables are tender, stirring twice.
2. Add bread crumbs, parsley, thyme, salt, and pepper to vegetable mixture. Stir to blend.
3. Spread half of the stuffing mixture in the center of each chicken breast. Roll up breasts and fold in the sides. Secure with a toothpick. Arrange roulades in a 10-inch round baking dish. Combine soup and wine and pour over chicken. Cover with wax paper. Microwave at power level HIGH for 11½ to 15 minutes, or until chicken is cooked. Let stand, covered, 3 to 5 minutes before serving.

Makes 2 servings.

Chicken Stew with Dumplings
(Recipe on page 40)

SHERRIED CHICKEN

2½ to 3 pounds chicken, cut into serving
    pieces
½ teaspoon salt
¼ teaspoon pepper
1 large onion, thinly sliced
⅓ cup dry sherry
1 tablespoon soy sauce
1 tablespoon lemon juice
1 tablespoon flour

1. Arrange chicken pieces in a 10-inch round baking dish, with meatier, thcker portions facing toward the outer edge of the dish. Sprinkle with salt and pepper and top with onion and bacon. Combine all remaining ingredients in a small bowl. Pour mixture evenly over chicken.
2. Cover chicken with wax paper. Microwave at power level HIGH for 16½ to 20 minutes, or until chicken is tender. Let stand, covered, 5 minutes before serving. Stir pan juices until smooth and spoon over chicken.

Makes 4 servings.

INDIAN CHICKEN

2 cups thinly sliced onion
2 tablespoon oil
2 tablespoons butter or margarine

2½ to 3 pounds chicken
1 teaspoon ground cumin
⅛ teaspoon cayenne pepper
½ teaspoon salt
¼ teaspoon pepper

2 tablespoons wine, chicken broth, or
    water
1 tablespoon cornstarch
½ teaspoon salt
½ cup slivered almonds, toasted
2 to 3 teaspoons lemon juice

1. Combine onion, oil, and butter in a 10-inch round baking dish. Microwave, uncovered, at power level HIGH for 6 to 9 minutes, or until onion is tender, stirring twice.
2. Add chicken, cumin, cayenne, salt, and pepper. Toss to blend. Cover with wax paper. Microwave at power level HIGH for 13 to 14 minutes. Let stand, covered, 5 minutes, then remove chicken to a serving platter.
3. Blend 2 tablespoons wine, chicken broth, or water with 1 tablespoon cornstarch. Stir this mixture into the pan juices. Add raisins and nuts. Microwave, uncovered, at power level HIGH for 4 to 5 minutes, or until sauce is thickened and bubbly, stirring 3 times. Flavor with lemon juice to taste. Spoon sauce over chicken and serve.

Makes 4 servings.

HAWAIIAN CHICKEN

2½ to 3 pounds chicken, cut into serving
    pieces
2 tablespoons soy sauce
1 tablespoon lemon juice
1 tablespoon packed dark brown sugar
½ teaspoon ground ginger
pinch cayenne pepper

1 11-ounce can mandarin oranges, drained,
    syrup reserved
1 8¼-ounce can pineapple chunks,
    drained, syrup reserved
3 tablespoons flour

1. Arrange chicken in a 10-inch round baking dish, with the thicker, meatier portions facing toward the outside of the dish. Combine soy sauce, lemon juice, brown sugar, ginger, and cayenne pepper. Brush mixture over chicken. Cover with wax paper. Microwave at power level HIGH for 13 minutes. Drain the chicken, reserving ½ cup of the juices.
2. Arrange chicken skin-side-up in baking dish. Cover with fruit. In a 4-cup glass measure or 1-quart bowl, combine reserved liquid from chicken, 1 cup syrup from fruits, and the flour. Blend until smooth. Pour this mixture over the chicken and stir. Cover chicken and microwave at power level LOW & DEFROST for 11 to 16 minutes, or until chicken is fully cooked and sauce is thickened, stirring once. Let stand, covered, 5 minutes before serving.

Makes 4 servings.

CHINESE CHICKEN WITH CASHEWS

3 tablespoons oil

2 chicken breasts, boned, skinned, and cut
   into ¾-inch cubes (1 to 1¼ lbs.)
2 cloves garlic, pressed or finely chopped
2 tablespoons soy sauce
1 tablespoon sherry
1 tablespoon cornstarch
½ to 1 teaspoon ground ginger
¼ teaspoon salt

1 green pepper, cut in ¾-inch cubes
⅔ cup cashews, halved

1. Pour oil into a 10-inch round baking dish and microwave, uncovered, at power level HIGH for 4 minutes.
2. While the oil is heating, combine all remaining ingredients, except
green pepper and cashews. Add chicken mixture to oil and microwave,
uncovered, at power level HIGH for 4 minutes, stirring twice.
3. Add green pepper and cashews. Cover. Microwave at power level
HIGH for 4 to 5 minutes, or until green pepper and chicken are cooked, stirring twice.
Let stand, covered, 2 to 3 minutes before serving.

Makes 3 to 4 servings.

CREAMY CHICKEN CASSEROLE

2 cups chopped cooked chicken
2 cups thinly sliced celery
½ cups slivered almonds, toasted
1 to 2 tablespoons greated onion
1 11-ounce can cream of mushroom soup
2 tablespoons dry while wine or dry sherry
1 tablespoon lemon juice

½ cup shredded process American cheese
1 cup crushed buttery crackers

1. Combine all ingredients, except cheese and crackers, in an 8-inch
round baking dish. Cover. Microwave at power level HIGH for 13 to
15 minutes, or until heated through, stirring twice.
2. Sprinkle first with cheese, then with crushed crackers. Microwave,
uncovered, at power level HIGH for 2½ minutes.

Makes 4 servings.

CHICKEN ENCHILADAS

⅓ cup chopped onion
1 tablespoon oil
½ cup chopped tomato
1 3-ounce can chopped green chilies,
   drained
2 cloves garlic, pressed or finely
   chopped
¼ teaspoon salt
1 cup chopped cooked chicken

4 6-inch flour tortillas
1 small avocado, peeled and pureed
¼ to ½ cup shredded Cheddar cheese

½ 8-ounce jar taco sauce, warmed

1. Combine onion and oil in a 1½-quart glass bowl. Microwave, uncovered, at power level HIGH for 6 minutes, stirring once. Add
tomato, chilies, garlic, and salt. Cover. Microwave at power level
HIGH for 6 minutes, stirring once. Drain if mixture seems watery. Add
chicken. Cover and microwave at power level HIGH for 4 to 5 minutes,
or until chicken is hot.
2. Wrap 4 tortillas in a damp towel or in damp paper toweling and
microwave at power level HIGH for ½ minutes, or until softened.
Spread about ¼ cup of the chicken filling on each tortilla and top with
a heaping tablespoon of pureed avocado. Roll tortilla around the filling. Repeat warming, filling, and rolling procedures with remaining
tortillas. Arrange filled tortillas seam-side-down on a 10-inch round
baking dish
3. Sprinkle tortillas with cheese. Microwave, uncovered, at power level
HIGH for 6 to 9 minutes, or until enchiladas are heated through. Serve
with any remaining pureed avocado and with warm taco sauce.

Makes 4 to 8 servings.

CHICKEN KABOBS

3 chicken breasts, boned, skinned, and cut
 into 1-inch chunks (1½ to 1¾ lbs.)
12 cherry tomatoes
2 small onions, quartered lengthwise
1 large green pepper, cut into 1-inch
 chunks

¼ cup oil, preferably olive oil
2 tablespoons soy sauce
2 tablespoons lemon juice
½ teaspoon whole thyme leaves
¼ teaspoon pepper

1. Thread chicken, tomatoes, onion quarters, and green pepper alternately on six 8-inch skewers. (Use wooden skewers if possible, though metal ones may also be used.) Arrange kabobs in a 10-inch round baking dish.
2. Combine all remaining ingredients in a small bowl. Brush on kabobs. Microwave, uncovered, at power level HIGH for 9 to 11½ minutes, or until chicken and vegetables are cooked, rearranging the skewers once and basting twice with marinade.

Makes 4 servings.

DEVILED CHICKEN LIVERS

8 tablespoons butter or margarine
6 tablespoons Dijon-style mustard
1 tablespoon very finely chopped green
 onion
1 tablespoon very finely chopped parsley
1 to 2 cloves garlic, pressed or finely
 chopped
2 teaspoons Worcestershire sauce
¼ teaspoon salt
¼ teaspoon pepper

1 pound chicken livers
1 cup fine dry bread crumbs

1. Place butter in a 4-cup glass measure and microwave at power level HIGH for 2½ to 4 minutes, or until melted. Pour 4 tablespoons of the melted butter into a 10-inch round baking dish and set aside. Combine the remaining 4 tablespoons butter with all ingredients, except chicken livers and crumbs. Blend well.
2. Cut the chicken livers in half, removing any large strings or green spots. Dip the chicken livers first in the mustard mixture, then in the bread crumbs. Arrange in the baking dish containing the melted butter, turning once to coat both sides with butter. Microwave, uncovered, at power level LOW & DEFROST for 11 to 14½ minutes, or until done to taste. Do not overcook. Livers taste best when firm but still pink inside.

Makes 4 servings.

ROAST GOOSE WITH APPLE STUFFING

1 cup thinly sliced celery
1 cup finely chopped onion
½ cup raisins
⅔ cup chicken broth
4 cups fresh bread crumbs
2 cups chopped apples
1 egg, lightly beaten
2 tablespoons finely chopped parsley
1 teaspoon rubbed sage
1 teaspoon salt
½ teaspoon pepper

8 pound goose
2 tablespoons instant beef broth dissolved
 in 4 tablespoons water

1. Combine clery, onion, raisins, and chicken broth in a 2½-quart glass bowl. Cover. Microwave at power level HIGH for 15 minutes, stirring twice. Add all remaining ingredients, except goose and dissolved beef broth. Blend well.
2. Stuff goose with apple mixture. Sew vent shut and tie wings and legs of bird to body. Pierce skin thoroughly with a sharp-tined fork. Place goose breast-side-down on a microwave-safe roasting rack set in a baking dish. Brush with dissolved beef broth. Microwave, uncovered, at power level LOW & DEFROST for 59 minutes. Drain off fat and turn bird over. Brush with dissolved beef broth. Microwave, uncovered, at power level LOW & DEFROST for 55 to 70 minutes, or until goose is tender, draining off fat once if necessary. Let stand, covered, 15 minutes before serving.

Makes 6 to 8 servings.

FRUITED CORNISH GAME HENS

2 1-pound Cornish game hens
1 cup sliced canned peaches, drained, syrup reserved
1 cup sliced canned pears, drained, syrup reserved
1 cup strong chicken broth
½ cup syrup from peaches and/or pears
2 tablespoons lemon juice
2 tablespoons cornstarch
1 teaspoon ground ginger

1. Arrange game hens breast-side-up in a 10-inch round baking dish. Cover with wax paper. Microwave at power level HIGH for 18 minutes, turning the game hens over after 7 minutes. Drain and turn hens breast-side-up again.
2. Combine remaining ingredients in a 1½-quart mixing bowl and blend well. Pour fruit mixture over game hens. Cover. Microwave at power level LOW & DEFROST for 16 to 19 minutes, or until sauce is thickened and poultry is fully cooked, stirring once. Let stand, covered, 5 minutes before serving.

Makes 4 servings.

STUFFED CORNISH GAME HENS

¾ cup orange juice
½ 6-ounce package long grain and wild rice mix
1 tablespoon butter or margarine
½ teaspoon rubbed sage or poultry seasoning
¼ cup slivered almonds, toasted

2 1-pound Cornish game hens
¼ cup orange juice concentrate
¼ cup honey
½ tablespoon instant beef bouillon

1. Combine orange juice, rice, butter, sage, and almonds in a 2-quart glass bowl. Cover. Set microwave oven at power level HIGH for 5 minutes, and then power level LOW & DEFROST for 20 minutes.
2. Stuff game hens with rice mixture. Sew vents shut. Tie legs and wings to the bodies. Combine orange juice concentrate, honey, and instant beef bouillon in a 2-cup glass measure. Microwave at power level HIGH for about 1½ minute, or until warmed. Stir to blend. Place stuffed game hens in a 10-inch round baking dish. Brush with orange-honey mixture. Cover with wax paper. Microwave at power level HIGH for 17 to 23 minutes, or until the meat near the bone is no longer pink. Brush every 6 minutes with orange-honey mixture. Let stand, covered, 10 minutes before serving.

Makes 2 to 4 servings.

TURKEY FLORENTINE

2 10-ounce packages frozen chopped spinach, thawed and pressed dry
2 to 3 cups cut-up or thinly sliced turkey
½ teaspoon salt
¼ teaspoon pepper
1 11-ounce can condensed cream of mushroom soup
3 tablespoons milk
2 tablespoons dry sherry

1. Place spinach in a 2½-quart glass casserole, covering the bottom of the dish evenly. Top with turkey and season with salt and pepper. Blend remaining ingredients until smooth in a small bowl. Pour mixture over turkey, smoothing with a spatula, if necessary.
2. Cover and microwave at power level HIGH for 10 to 13 minutes, or until heated through. Let stand, covered, 5 minutes before serving.

Makes 4 servings.

BEER-BARBECUED TURKEY DRUMSTICKS

2½ to 3 pounds turkey drumsticks,
 defrosted
1 cup barbecue sauce
½ cup beer
1 tablespoon packed dark brown sugar
1 teaspoon ground ginger
¼ teaspoon salt
¼ teaspoon pepper

1. Arrange drumsticks in a 10-inch round baking dish, with meatier, thicker portions facing the outside edge of the dish. Combine all remaining ingredients in a small bowl and pour mixture over turkey. Cover.

2. Microwave at power level HIGH for 15 minutes., Turn drumsticks over. Cover and microwave at power level LOW & DEFROST for 65 to 75 minutes, or until meat is tender. Serve drumsticks with sauce in the dish.

Makes 4 servings.

ORANGE-GLAZED DUCK

¼ cup frozen orange juice concentrate
⅓ cup water or fruit juice
1 beef bouillon cube
1 tablespoon packed dark brown sugar
¼ teaspoon pepper

4-to 5-pounds duck

1. Combine all ingredients, except duck, in a 2-cup glass measure. Microwave, uncovered, at power level HIGH for 3 to 4 minutes, or until mixture is hot, stirring twice. Set aside.

2. Pull large lumps of fat from the front cavity of the duck and pierce the skin thoroughly with a fork. Place duck breast-side-down on a microwavesafe roasting rack set on a round baking dish. Microwave, uncovered, at power level LOW & DEFROST for 48 minutes. Drain off fat.

3. Turn duck breast side up and brush with orange glaze. Microwave, uncovered, at power level LOW & DEFROST for 40 to 55 minutes, or until duck is no longer pink near the bones. Brush every 10 minutes with orange glaze. Let stand, covered, 10 minutes before serving.

Makes 4 servings.

Notes

FISH & SHELLFISH

Baked Red Snapper Meuniere
(Recipe on page 49)

POACHED FISH FILLETS

4 fish fillets (1 to 1¼ pounds altogether)
½ cup dry white wine or tomato juice
3 tablespoons butter, cut into ¼-inch pieces
2 tablespoons finely chopped green onion
¼ teaspoon salt
¼ teaspoon pepper

1. Fold fillets in half and arrange in a small, shallow baking dish, with thicker portions facing the outside edge of the dish. Pour wine over fish. Dot with butter and sprinkle on chopped onion, salt, and pepper. Cover.
2. Microwave at power level HIGH for 5 to 7½ minutes, or until fish flakes when prodded with a fork. Let stand, covered, 3 to 5 minutes, or until fish becomes white and firm all the way through.

Makes 4 servings.

FLOUNDER WITH SHRIMP SAUCE

4 flounder fillets (about 1 pound altogether)
1 11-ounce can condensed cream of shrimp soup
1 3½-ounce can small shrimp, drained
1 2½-ounce can mushrooms, drained
¼ cup white wine or milk
1 tablespoon dried parsley flakes
¼ teaspoon salt
¼ teaspoon pepper, preferably white pepper

1. Roll up flounder fillets and arrage fillets seam-side-down in an 8-inch round baking dish. Combine all remaining ingredients in a small bowl. Spoon shrimp mixture over fillets. Cover.
2. Microwave at power level HIGH for 7½ to 9 minutes, or until fish is firm to the touch. Let stand, covered, 5 minutes before serving.

Makes 4 servigs.

TROUT AMONDINE

8 tablespoons (1 stick) butter
½ to ⅔ cup shaved almonds

2 whole trout, cleaned (about 12 ounces each)
2 teaspoons lemon juice
¼ teaspoon salt
¼ teaspoon pepper

1. Combine butter and almonds in a 2-cup glass measure. Microwave, uncovered, at power level HIGH for 4 to 6 minutes. or until almonds are lightly browned, stirring twice.
2. Season trout with lemon juice, salt, and pepper. Arrange in a 10-inch round baking dish. Pour almond-butter mixture over trout and inside cavities. Cover with wax paper. Microwave at power level HIGH for 6 to 9 minutes, or until fish flakes. Let stand, covered, 5 minutes before serving.

Makes 2 servings.

BAKED RED SNAPPER MEUNIERE

8 tablespoons (1 stick) butter, cut into thin pats
¼ cup finely chopped parsley
1 tablespoon lemon juice

2½-to 3-pounds snapper, whole or pan-dressed

1. In a 10-inch round baking dish, combine butter, parsley, and lemon juice. Microwave, uncovered, at power level HIGH for 1½ to 2½ minutes, or until butter is melted. Stir to combine ingredients.
2. Place snapper in baking dish, turning once to coat both sides with butter mixture. Cover with wax paper. Microwave at power level HIGH for 10 to 13½ minutes, turning the fish over with large spatulas after 5 minutes' cooking time. The fish is done when the flesh comes away easily from the bones when flaked with a fork. Let fish stand, covered, for 3 to 5 minutes before serving.

Makes 3 to 4 servings.

HALIBUT DIVAN

1 pound halibut fillets
1 10-ounce package frozen broccoli spears, thawed
1 11-ounce cream of shrimp soup
2 teaspoons lemon juice
¼ teaspoon salt
¼ teaspoon pepper, preferably white pepper

1. Arrange halibut in a 10-inch round baking dish, with thicker, meatier portions facing toward the outer edge of the dish. Lay broccoli spears on top, with flowerets facing outward. Cover dish with plastic wrap. Microwave at power level HIGH for 10 to 13 minutes, or until fish flakes easily and broccoli is crisp-tender. Let stand, covered, for 3 minutes.

2. In a 4-cup glass measure, blend all remaining ingredients. After fish has stood 3 minutes, drain juices into soup mixture. Microwave sauce at power level HIGH for 4 to 5 minutes, or until hot, stirring twice. Stir in any further juices from fish. Turn fish onto serving platter and spoon sauce on top.

Makes 4 servings.

SEAFOOD NEWBURG

1 11-ounce can condensed cream of mushroom soup
1 10-ounce package frozen peas, thawed
1 2½-ounce jar mushrooms, drained
2 tablespoons very finely chopped onion
¼ cup milk or half-and-half
big pinch cayenne pepper
¼ teaspoon salt
¼ teaspoon pepper
1 pound cooked seafood, cut into bite-size pieces
2 to 3 tablespoons sherry

1. Combine all ingredients, except seafood and sherry, in a 1½-quart glass casserole. Blend well. Cover. Microwave at power level HIGH for 5 to 6 minutes, or until heated, stirring once.

2. Add shrimp and sherry to mushroom mixture. Cover. Microwave at power level LOW & DEFROST for 8 to 9½ minutes, or until heated through, stirring once. Let stand, covered, 5 minutes before serving.

Makes 3 to 4 servings.

PAELLA

2 small chicken breasts, boned and cut into strips (¾ to 1 pound)
½ pound hot Italian sausage, crumbled, casings removed
½ cup chopped onion

1½ cups chicken broth
⅔ cup uncooked long-grain rice
1 large tomato, peeled, seeded, and chopped
1 clove garlic, pressed or finely chopped
½ teaspoon oregano
¼ teaspoon ground dried orange peel (optional)
¼ teaspoon saffron, crushed
¼ teaspoon salt
½ teaspoon pepper

12 shrimp in shells
4 small clams in shells

1. Combine chicken, sausage, and onion in a 2-quart glass casserole. Microwave, uncovered, at power level HIGH for 9 minutes, stirring once. Drain off fat.

2. Add remaining ingredients, except seafood. Cover. Microwave at power level LOW & DEFROST for 32 minutes, or until rice is tender, stirring every 5 minutes.

3. Place seafood on top of rice mixture. Cover. Microwave at power level LOW & DEFROST for 4½ to 8 minutes, or until seafood is cooked.

Makes 4 servings.

SHRIMP SCAMPI

8 tablespoons (1 stick) butter or margarine
3 to 6 cloves garlic, pressed or finely
  chopped
2 tablespoons lemon juice
2 tablespoons dried parsley flakes
½ teaspoon salt
¼ teaspoon pepper

1 pound shrimp, shelled

1. In a shallow baking dish, combine all ingredients except for shrimp. Microwave, uncovered, at power level HIGH for 4 to 5 minutes, or until hot, stirring twice.
2. Stir shrimp into butter sauce. Cover. Microwave at power level HIGH for 5 to 7½ minutes, or until shrimp curl and turn pink. Let stand, covered, 3 to 5 minutes before serving.

Makes 4 servings.

CREOLE SHRIMP

½ cup finely chopped onion
½ cup finely chopped green pepper
¼ cup finely chopped celery
¼ cup oil, preferably olive oil

1 cup thick tomato sauce
1 pound medium shrimp, shelled
2 to 3 cloves garlic, pressed or finely
  chopped
¾ teaspoon salt
¼ teaspoon pepper

1. Combine onion, green pepper, celery, and oil in a 2-quart glass casserole. Microwave, uncovered, at power level HIGH for 6 minutes, or until the vegetables are crisp-tender, stirring once.
2. Add all remaining ingredients. Cover. Set microwave oven at power level HIGH for 5 minutes, and then power level LOW & DEFROST for 4½ minutes. Stir twice during cooking. Let stand, covered, 3 minutes before serving.

Makes 4 servings.

SCALLOPS ST. JACQUES

3 tablespoons butter
3 talespoons flour
1½ cups light cream or half-and-half
⅓ cup dry sherry
½ teaspoon salt
¼ teaspoon pepper, preferably white pepper

3 tablespoons butter
1 pound scallops, halved or quartered
  lengthwise if large
1 cup sliced fresh mushrooms
1 teaspoon lemon juice

1. In a 4-cup glass measure, melt 3 tablespoons butter by microwaving at power level HIGH for 1½ to 2½ minutes. Stir in flour, making a smooth paste. Add cream. Microwave, uncovered, at power level HIGH for 5½ to 7 minutes, or until mixture boils and becomes very thick, stirring twice. Stir in sherry, salt, and pepper. Set mixture aside.
2. Place remaining 3 tablespoons butter in a 2-quart glass casserole and microwave at power level HIGH for 1½ to 2½ minutes, or until melted. Stir in scallops, mushrooms, and lemon juice. Cover. Microwave at power level HIGH for 4 to 5 minutes, or until mushrooms and scallops are tender, stirring every minute. Fold in reserved cream sauce. If necessary, reheat by microwaving at power level HIGH for 1½ minutes. If desired, serve in individual scallop shells or over rice.

Makes 4 servings.

ONIONY TUNA CASSEROLE

2 7-ounce cans tuna fish, undrained
2 11-ounce cans condensed cream of onion
  soup
2 to 3 cups cooked pasta
1 4-ounce can sliced mushrooms, undrained
2 tablespoons lemon juice
¼ teaspoon ground thyme
¼ teaspoon salt
½ teaspoon pepper

1 3½-ounce can French-fried onion rings

1. Combine tuna and soup in a 2-quart glass casserole, breaking up tuna slightly. Add all remaining ingredients, except onion rings. Cover.
2. Microwave at power level HIGH for 13½ to 17 minutes, or until hot, stirring twice. Let stand, covered, 3 minutes. Top with onion rings before serving.

Makes 4 to 6 servings.

SALMON QUICHE

3 eggs
1 cup milk
15 to 16 ounces canned salmon
1 4½-ounce jar mushrooms, drained
2 tablespoons finely chopped green onion
2 tablespoons finely chopped parsley
1 cup shredded Cheddar cheese
big pinch cayenne pepper
½ teaspoon salt
1 9-inch baked pastry shell in a glass pie
  dish (recipe on page 87)

1. Beat eggs and milk together until blended. Add salmon, breaking up lightly with a fork. Gently stir in remaining ingredients. Pour mixture into baked pie shell, being sure the solids are distributed evenly in the bottom of the shell.
2. Microwave, uncovered, at power level HIGH for 10½ to 13½ minutes. Let stand for 5 to 10 minutes, or until center becomes firm.

Makes 4 to 6 servings.

MARYLAND CRAB CASSEROLE

1 cup chopped celery
1 cup chopped onion
1 cup chopped green pepper
4 tablespoons butter or margarine

12 ounces crabmeat, canned and drained
  or frozen and thawed
1 cup mayonnaise
4 hard-cooked eggs, chopped
1 teaspoon Worcestershire sauce
½ teaspoon salt
¼ teaspoon pepper

1 cup buttery cracker crumbs
2 tablespoons butter or margarine, melted

1. Combine celery, onion, green pepper, and 4 tablespoons butter in a 2-quart glass casserole. Microwave, uncovered, at power level HIGH for 5 to 7½ minutes, or until vegetables are tender.
2. Stir in remaining ingredients, except cracker crumbs and last 2 tablespoons melted butter. Blend well. Cover. Microwave at power level LOW & DEFROST for 11 to 14½ minutes, or until heated through, stirring twice.
3. Combine cracker crumbs and melted butter. Sprinkle over casserole. Let stand 5 minutes before serving.

Makes 4 servings.

BAKED STUFFED CLAMS

3 tablespoons olive oil
3 slices bacon, cut up
¼ cup finely chopped onion
⅔ cup fine dry bread crumbs
2 to 3 tablespoons finely chopped parsley
1 to 2 cloves garlic, pressed or finely
   chopped
¼ teaspoon ground thyme
¼ teaspoon paprika
big pinch cayenne pepper
¼ teaspoon salt
¼ teaspoon pepper

18 small clams (little necks), scrubbed,
   opened, and on the half shell

1. Combine olive oil, bacon, and onion in a 1-quart glass casserole. Microwave, uncovered, at power level HIGH for 4 to 6 minutes, or until bacon is crisp. Add all remaining ingredients, except clams, and blend well.

2. Arrange clams around the edge of a 10-inch glass pizza dish. Pierce each clam several times with a toothpick. Top clams with crumb mixture. Microwave, uncovered, at power level HIGH for 5½ to 7 minutes, or until clams are cooked.

Makes 3 to 4 servings.

Notes

VEGETABLES

Green Beans Almondine
(Recipe on page 56)

TIPS ON COOKING FRESH AND FROZEN VEGETABLES

- Pierce the skins of whole potatoes, sweet potatoes, eggplants, and winter squash before proceeding to microwave. This allows steam to escape and prevents the vegetables from bursting in the oven.
- Fresh vegetables should be cooked in a covered glass casserole or baking dish. Add 2 to 4 tablespoons water per pound of vegetable.
- Frozen vegetables may be cooked in thier original carton, provided the carton has no metallic or foil parts, or in plastic cooking pouch. Vegetables in a carton should be laid on a double thickness of paper toweling, which will absorb moisture. Cooking pouches should be slit to allow steam to escape. Check microwave directions on carton.
- For best results, stir vegetables frequently and check for doneness every minute or so. Overcooked vegetables are a kitchen disaster.
- Most vegetables should be allowed to stand 3 to 5 minutes to complete cooking. Bright green vegetables, however, such as beans, peas, and Brussels sprouts, should be microwaved until tender and served at once.
- Check chart for cooking and standing times for various vegetables.

VEGETABLE COOKING TABLE

VEGETABLE	PREPARATION	AMOUNT	COOKING TIME AT POWER LEVEL 11	STANDING TIME
artichokes, fresh	whole	4 (8 oz., ea.)	15-19 minutes	5 minutes
artichokes, frozen	hearts	9-oz. package	9-13 minutes	5 minutes
asparagus, fresh	1½-in. pieces	1 lb.	6-7 minutes	3 minutes
asparagus, frozen	whole spears	10-oz. package	7½-10 minutes	3 minutes
beans, green or wax, fresh	1½-in. pieces	1 lb.	8-10 minutes	—
beans, green or wax, frozen	cut up	9-oz. package	7½-10 minutes	3 minutes
beets, fresh,	sliced	1½-2 lbs.	14-16½ minutes	5 minutes
broccoil, fresh	spears	1 lb.	7½-10 minutes	—
broccoli, frozen	whole or cut	10-oz. package	8-10 minutes	3 minutes
Brussels sprouts, fresh	whole	10-oz. tub	7-9 minutes	—
Brussels sprouts, frozen	whole	10-oz. package	9½-12 minutes	3 minutes
cabbage, fresh	chopped	1 lb.	8-10 minutes	5 minutes
	wedges	1 lb.	9-11½ minutes	5 minutes
carrots, fresh	½-in. slices	1 lb.	10-13 minutes	3 minutes
carrots, frozen	sliced	10-oz. package	7-9 minutes	3 minutes
cauliflower, fresh	flowerets	1 medium head	8-10 minutes	3 minutes
	whole	1 medium head	13-19 minutes	5 minutes
cauliflower, frozen	flowerets	10-oz. package	7-9 minutes	3 minutes
celery, fresh	½-in. slices	1 lb.	13-15 minutes	5 minutes
corn, fresh	on cob, husked	4 ears	13-15 minutes	5 minutes
corn, frozen	on cob, husked	4 ears	14-16½ minutes	5 minutes
	whole kernel	10-oz package	5-7 minutes	3 minutes
eggplant, fresh	cubed	1 lb.	9-10 minutes	3 minutes
	whole, pierced	1-1¼ lbs.	6-10 minutes	5 minutes
leeks, fresh	whole, ends	1 lb.	12-13 minutes	5 minutes
lima beans, frozen	whole	10-oz. package	7-9 minutes	3 minutes
mixed vegetables, frozen	—	10-oz. package	8-10 minutes	3 minutes
mushrooms, fresh	sliced	1 lb.	5-7½ minutes	3 minutes
okra, frozen	sliced	10-oz. package	6-8 minutes	5 minutes
onions, fresh	whole, peeled	8-10 small	13-19 minutes	5 minutes
peas, fresh	shelled	1 lbs.	6-9 minutes	—
peas, frozen	shelled	10-oz. package	7-9 minutes	3 minutes
pea pods (snow peas), frozen	whole	6-oz. package	5-6 minutes	—
peas and carrots	—	10-oz. package	7-9 minutes	3 minutes
peas, black-eyed, frozen	whole	10-oz. package	25-29 minutes	5 minutes
parsnips, fresh	cubed	1 lb.	10-13 minutes	5 minutes
potatoes, white or sweet, fresh	whole	4 (6 oz. ea.)	13-15 minutes	3 minutes
	whole	8 (6 oz. ea.)	20-22 minutes	5 minutes
rutablaga, fresh	cubed	4 cups	15-17 minutes	5 minutes
spinach, fresh	whole leaf	1 lb.	6-7½ minutes	—
spinach, frozen	leaf of chopped	10-oz. package	8-10 minutes	3 minutes
squash, summer, fresh	½-in. slices	1 lb.	7½-9 minutes	3 minutes
squash, summer, frozen	sliced	10-oz. package	6-8 minutes	3 minutes
squash, winter, fresh	whole, pierced	1½ lbs.	15-19 minutes	5 minutes
squash, winter, frozen	whipped	12-oz. package	8-10 minutes	3 minutes
succotash, frozen	—	10-oz. package	7-9 minutes	3 minutes
turnips, fresh,	cubed	4 cups	13-15 minutes	3 minutes

GREEN BEANS ALMONDINE

⅓ cup slivered or shaved almonds
4 tablespoons butter or margarine

1½ pounds fresh green beans, halved
⅓ cup water
1 teaspoon lemon juice
½ teaspoon salt
¼ teaspoon pepper

1. Combine almonds and butter in a 2-cup glass measure. Microwave, uncovered, at power level HIGH for 4 to 6 minutes, or until almonds are lightly toasted. Set aside.
2. Combine beans and water in a 2-quart glass casserole. Cover. Microwave at power level HIGH for 10 to 13 minutes, or until beans are crisp-tender. Drain. Toss beans with reserved almond-butter mixture and all remaining ingredients.

Makes 4 to 6 servings.

CORN ON THE COB

4 ears corn on the cob

1. Place unhusked ears of corn directly on the floor of the oven, leaving space in between. Microwave, uncovered, at power level HIGH for 15 to 19 minutes, depending on the size of the ears. Turn over the ears every 4 minutes. Let stand 5 minutes.
2. To remove husk, grasp corn at the base of the ear, using a napkin to protect your hand. With your free hand, gradually pull back the husk at the tip of the ear, allowing the steam to escape before continuing to strip off the rest of the husk. Remove silk by grasping firmly with your hand or by brushing away with a napkin.

Makes 4 servings.

SUCCOTASH

1 10-ounce package frozen lima beans
1 10-ounce package frozen whole kernel corn
2 tablespoons chopped pimento (optional)
1 teaspoon dried parsley flakes (optional)

4 tablespoons butter or margarine
½ teaspoon salt
⅛ teaspoon pepper

1. Combine limas, corn, pimento, and parsley flakes in a 2-quart glass casserole. Cover. Microwave at power level HIGH for 11½ to 14 minutes, or until vegetables are tender, stirring twice.
2. Add remaining ingredients. Microwave, covered, at power level HIGH for 2½ minutes.

Makes 4 to 6 servings.

BROCCOLI IN EGG SAUCE

2 10-ounce packages frozen chopped broccoli, thawed and well drained
1 11-ounce can condensed cream of mushroom soup
4 hard-cooked eggs, chopped
¼ cup whipping cream
1 tablespoon sherry (optional)
big pinch ground nutmeg
big pinch cayenne pepper
¼ teaspoon salt
¼ teaspoon pepper, preferably white pepper

½ cup shredded Swiss cheese
⅓ cup fine dry bread crumbs
2 tablespoons butter, cut into ¼-inch pieces

1. Combine broccoli and soup in a 2-quart glass casserole. Gently stir in eggs, whipping cream, sherry, and seasonings. Cover. Microwave at power level HIGH for 13 to 15 minutes, or until hot, stirring twice.
2. Top casserole with Swiss cheese, crumbs, and pieces of butter. Microwave, uncovered, at power level HIGH for 3½ minutes. Let stand 2 to 3 minutes before serving.

Makes 6 servings.

MUSTARD-TOPPED CAULIFLOWER

1 medium head cauliflower
⅓ cup water

½ cup mayonnaise
1 tablespoon finely chopped onion
2 teaspoons prepared mustard
¼ teaspoon salt
⅔ cup shredded Cheddar or Swiss cheese
¼ teaspoon paprika (optional)

1. Place cauliflower in deep casserole and add water. Cover. Microwave at power level HIGH for 13 to 19 minutes, or until cauliflower is tender. Drain.
2. Combine all remaining ingredients, except cheese and paprika. Spoon mixture over cauliflower, then sprinkle with cheese and paprika. Microwave, uncovered, at power level HIGH for 2 to 2½ minutes, or until cheese is melted.

Makes 6 servings.

CREAMED SPINACH

2 10-ounce packages frozen chopped spinach, thawed and well drained
2 tablespoons butter
2 tablespoons finely chopped green onion

1½ tablespoons flour
1 cup whipping cream
⅛ teaspoon ground nutmeg
½ teaspoon salt
¼ teaspoon pepper

1. Combine spinach, butter, and onion in a 1½-quart glass casserole. Cover and microwave at power level HIGH for 4½ minutes, or until spinach is very hot, stirring twice.
2. Stir flour into spinach, blending until smooth. Stir in remaining ingredients. Microwave, uncovered, at power level HIGH for 5 to 6 minutes, or until mixture boils and thickens, stirring twice. Let stand, covered, 5 minutes before serving.

Makes 4 to 6 servings.

GINGERY CARROTS

1 pound carrots, scraped and cut into ¼-inch slices
⅓ cup orange juice
2 tablespoons honey
½ teaspoon ground ginger
¼ teaspoon salt

1 tablespoon cornstarch
2 tablespoons orange juice

1. Combine all ingredients, except cornstarch and last 2 tablespoons orange juice, in a 1½-quart glass casserole. Cover. Microwave at power level HIGH for 10 to 13 minutes, or until carrots are tender, stirring twice.
2. Combine cornstarch and 2 tablespoons orange juice and blend into carrots. Microwave, uncovered, at power level HIGH for 1½ to 2½ minutes, or until thickened, stirring once.

Makes 4 servings.

MASHED POTATOES

2 pounds potatoes, peeled and quartered
2 tablespoons water

⅔ cup half-and-half or milk
4 tablespoons butter or margarine
½ to ¾ teaspoon salt
¼ teaspoon pepper, preferably white pepper

1. Place potatoes in a 2-quart glass bowl. Sprinkle on water. Cover. Microwave at power level HIGH for 10 to 13 minutes, or until potatoes are tender, stirring twice. Let stand, covered, 5 minutes. Drain off liquid. Turn potatoes into a ricer and force through ricer back into casserole. Cover and set aside.
2. Heat all remaining ingredients in a 2-cup glass measure by microwaving, uncovered, at power level HIGH for 2½ to 4 minutes. Gradually pour milk mixture into riced potatoes while beating potatoes with a wire whip or electric beater. If necessary, reheat mashed potatoes by covering and microwaving at power level HIGH for 2½ to 4 minutes.

Makes 6 servings.

RICH STUFFED BAKED POTATOES

4 medium baking potatoes

4 tablespoons butter or margarine
⅓ cup milk or half-and-half
¼ cup crumbled bacon or snipped chives
    (optional)
¼ cup shredded Swiss cheese
¼ cup grated Parmesan cheese
¼ to ½ teaspoon, salt
¼ teaspoon pepper

1. Pierce potatoes well with a fork and place on the floor of the oven. Microwave, uncovered, at power level HIGH for 13 to 19 minutes, or until tender, rearranging and turning potatoes over after 6 minutes' cooking time. Let stand 3 minutes.
2. Cut potatoes in half, scoop out cooked potato from shells, and combine potato with butter in a 1½-quart mixing bowl. Add milk and mash lightly; the potatoes should remain somewhat lumpy. Stir in all remaining ingredients. Fill potato shells with mashed potatoes and place on a microwave-safe serving platter. Microwave, uncovered, at power level HIGH for 4½ to 5½ minutes, or until heated through. Let stand 3 minutes before serving.

Makes 4 to 8 servings.

RICH POTATOES WITH CHEESE

3 slices bacon
⅓ cup chopped onion

1 cup shredded Cheddar cheese
½ cup cream-style cottage cheese
1 tablespoon finely chopped parsley
¼ teaspoon salt
⅛ teaspoon pepper
3 cups cubed potatoes, cut in ½ inch cubes

¼ cup fine dry bread crumbs
¼ cup grated Parmesan cheese
1½ tablespoons butter or margarine, cut
    into small pieces

1. Arrange bacon in a single layer in a 2-quart glass casserole. Microwave, uncovered, at power level HIGH for 4 to 5 minutes, or until crisp. Remove bacon, crumble, and set aside. Add onion to drippings. Microwave, uncovered, at power level HIGH for 3 minutes, or until tender, stirring twice. Stir in crumbled bacon.
2. Add Cheddar cheese, cottage cheese, parsley, salt, and pepper to casserole. Stir to blend. Fold in potatoes. Cover. Microwave at power level HIGH for 9 to 10½ minutes, or until almost tender, stirring twice.
3. Stir again then sprinkle crumbs and grated Parmesan cheese on casserole and top with pieces of butter. Microwave, uncovered, at power level HIGH for 3½ minutes.

Makes 4 servings.

SWEET POTATO CASSEROLE DELUXE

1 17-ounce can vacuum-packed sweet
    potatoes or yams
1 16-ounce can sliced peaches, undrained
¼ cup packed dark brown sugar
4 tablespoons butter or margarine, cut into
    pats
2 tablespoons rum, brandy, or sweet sherry
1 tablespoon grated orange peel
½ teaspoon salt

1. Combine all ingredients in a 2-quart glass casserole. Cover.
2. Microwave at power level HIGH for 10 to 13½ minutes, or until hot and bubbly, stirring twice. Let stand, covered, 3 to 5 minutes before serving.

Makes 4 to 6 servings.

HONEYED WINTER SQUASH

2 pounds acorn, butternut, hubbard, or
    other winter squash, peeled and cut into
    1-inch cubes (about 4 cups)
6 tablespoons butter or margarine
⅓ cup honey
½ teaspoon rubbed sage
½ teaspoon salt
¼ teaspoon pepper

1. Combine all ingredients in a 2-quart glass casserole. Cover.
2. Microwave at power level HIGH for 13 to 15 minutes, or until squash is tender, stirring twice. Let stand, covered, 3 minutes before serving.

Makes 4 to 6 servings.

SPICY BARBECUE BEANS

2 16-ounce cans pork and beans in tomato
   sauce
4 slices bacon, cut up
¼ cup barbecue sauce
¼ cup finely chopped onion
¼ cup packed dark brown sugar or
   molasses
1 teaspoon dry mustard
1 teaspoon chili powder
⅛ teaspoon ground cloves or allspice
¼ teaspoon salt
½ teaspoon pepper

1. Combine all ingredients in a 1½-quart glass casserole. Cover.
2. Microwave at power level HIGH for 20½ minutes, or until bubbly, stirring 3 times. Let stand, covered, 5 minutes before serving.

Makes 6 servings.

SPICED CABBAGE

4 tablespoons butter or margarine
1 small head cabbage, cored and cut into 6
   wedges (about 1½ pounds)

¼ cup chili sauce
2 tablespoons water
½ teaspoon caraway seeds
⅛ teaspoon ground cloves or allspice
½ teaspoon salt
¼ teaspoon pepper

1. Place butter in a 10-inch round baking dish. Microwave, uncovered, at power level HIGH for 1½ to 2½ minutes, or until melted. Roll cabbage wedges in melted butter to coat. Arrange cabbage so that the wider portion of the wedges faces the outside of the dish.
2. Combine all remaining ingredients in a small bowl. Spoon evenly over the cabbage wedges. Cover. Microwave at power level HIGH for 13 to 15 minutes, or until cabbage is nearly tender. Let stand, covered, 5 minutes before serving to complete cooking.

Makes 6 servings.

ZUCCHINI CASSEROLE

6 slices bacon
1 cup chopped onion

4 medium zucchini, cut into ½-inch slices
   (about 1½ pounds)
1 cup thick tomato sauce
1 clove garlic, pressed or finely chopped
1 teaspoon oregano
½ teaspoon salt
¼ teaspoon pepper

1 cup shredded mozzarella cheese

1. Arrange bacon in a single layer in a 10-inch round baking dish. Microwave, uncovered, at power level HIGH for 6 to 7½ minutes, or until crisp. Remove bacon and crumble. Add onion to drippings. Microwave, uncovered, at power level HIGH for 6 minutes, or until nearly tender, stirring twice. Stir in crumbled bacon.
2. Add all remaining ingredients, except cheese, and stir to blend. Cover. Microwave at power level HIGH for 9 to 11½ minutes, or until zucchini is tender, stirring twice.
3. Sprinkle casserole with mozzarella cheese. Cover and let stand 5 minutes before serving.

Makes 4 servings.

Eggplant Casserole
(Recipe on page 61)

RATATOUILLE

½ cup thinly sliced onion
⅓ cup chopped green pepper
¼ cup olive oil

1 medium eggplant, peeled and cut into
  ½-inch cubes (about 1 pound)
½ cup thick tomato sauce
1 to 2 cloves garlic, pressed or finely
  chopped
1 teaspoon basil
½ teaspoon oregano or whole thyme leaves
¼ teaspoon ground dried orange peel
  (optional)
½ teaspoon salt
⅛ teaspoon pepper

1. Combine onion, green pepper, and oil in a 2-quart casserole. Microwave, uncovered, at power level HIGH for 5 minutes, or until vegetables are nearly tender, stirring twice.
2. Add all remaining ingredients and stir to blend. Cover. Microwave at power level HIGH for 15 to 18 minutes, or until all vegetables are tender, stirring 3 or 4 times. Let stand, covered, 10 minutes before serving.

Makes 3 to 4 servings.

EGGPLANT CASSEROLE

1 medium eggplant (about 1 pound)
1 8-ounce can tomato sauce
⅓ cup grated Parmesan cheese
1½ tablespoons oil, preferably olive oil
1 clove garlic, pressed or finely chopped
½ teaspoon oregano
⅛ teaspoon pepper

1 cup shredded Swiss cheese

1. Peel eggplant, removing stem and cap, and cut eggplant in ¼-inch widthwise slices. Set aside. Mix together all remaining ingredients, except Swiss cheese, in a 1-quart mixing bowl. Cover the bottom of a 2-quart casserole with ⅔ cup of the tomato sauce mixture. Add a layer of sliced eggplant and cover with an additional ½ cup sauce. Make two more layers of eggplant, each of them topped with ½ cup sauce.
2. Cover casserole and microwave at power level HIGH for 10 to 13 minutes. Sprinkle with cheese and microwave, uncovered, at power level HIGH for 3 minutes, longer. Let stand 3 minutes before serving.

Makes 2 to 3 servings.

ITALIAN ARTICHOKES

¼ cup oil, preferably olive oil
2 to 3 cloves garlic, pressed or finely
  chopped
1 16-ounce can tomatoes, drained, seeded,
  and chopped
1 teaspoon oregano
¾ teaspoon salt
¼ teaspoon pepper

4 medium artichokes
½ lemon

1. Combine oil and garlic in a 2-quart glass casserole. Microwave, uncovered, at power level HIGH for 4 minutes, stirring once. Stir in tomatoes, oregano, salt, and pepper. Microwave, uncovered, at power level HIGH for 5 minutes, or until hot, stirring once.
2. Slice stems artichokes Snip off thorny tips of the leaves with kitchen shears. Slice off about 1½ inches of the top of the vegetables. Rub cut surfaces of the artichokes with the lemon half. Arrange artichokes in a circle in the casserole containing the tomato sauce, spooning some of the sauce on top of the artichokes. Cover with plastic wrap. Microwave at power level HIGH for 15 to 19 minutes, or until the base of the artichokes is tender when pierced with a fork. Let stand, covered 3 to 5 minutes before serving. Accompany with sauce in the casserole.

Makes 4 servings.

ASPARAGUS PARMESAN

1 10-ounce package frozen asparagus

1½ tablespoons butter, or margarine, cut
    into small pieces
⅓ cup grated Parmesan cheese
⅛ teaspoon pepper

1. Place asparagus in a 2-quart casserole. Cover. Microwave at power level HIGH for about 6 to 8 minutes, or until asparagus is tender, separating the asparagus. Drain well.
2. Sprinkle pieces of butter over asparagus and gently tilt the dish to coat asparagus with butter. Sprinkle with Parmesan cheese and pepper. Microwave, uncovered, at power level HIGH for 2 minutes. Let stand 2 to 3 minutes before serving.

Makes 2 to 3 servings.

SNOW PEAS WITH ALMONDS & MUSHROOMS

2 cups sliced fresh mushrooms
½ cup chopped green onion, including the
    tender part of the green tops
4 tablespoons butter or margarine

1 tablespoon cornstarch
1 tablespoon instant chicken bouillon
1 tablespoon soy sauce
1 tablespoon dry white wine or water

2 6-ounce packages frozen snow peas
   (pea pods), thawed
⅓ cup toasted slivered or shaved almonds

1. Combine mushrooms, green onion, and butter in a 2-quart glass casserole. Cover. Microwave at power level HIGH for 9 minutes, stirring twice.
2. Blend cornstarch, instant bouillon, soy sauce, and white wine in a 1-cup measure. Pour mixture into mushrooms and stir. Microwave, uncovered, at power level HIGH for 4 to 5 minutes, or until mixture is bubbly and thickened, stirring twice.
3. Stir snow peas into mushroom mixture. Microwave, uncovered, at power level HIGH for 2 to 2½ minutes, or until heated through, stirring twice. Fold in toasted almonds.

Makes 4 to 6 servings.

BRAISED CELERY

8 ribs celery, cut into 3-inch lengths
1½ cups sliced fresh mushrooms
½ cup chopped onion
1 11-ounce can condensed beef broth
2 tablespoons butter
1 tablespoon dried parsley flakes
½ teaspoon whole thyme leaves
¼ teaspoon pepper

2 tablespoons white wine or water
1 tablespoon cornstarch

1. Place all ingredients, except cornstarch and white wine, in a 2-quart glass casserole. Cover. Set microwave oven at power level HIGH for 6 minutes, and then power level HIGH for 18 minutes. Stir occasionally.
2. Combine white wine and cornstarch. Stir mixture into the celery. Microwave, uncovered, at power level HIGH for 1½ to 2½ minutes, or until sauce thickens, stirring once.

Makes 4 servings.

BRAISED GREEN PEPPERS

6 large green peppers
3 cloves garlic, pressed or finely chopped
¼ cup olive oil

1. Cut peppers in half lengthwise and remove seeds, ribs, and stems. Place in a 3-quart casserole and sprinkle with garlic. Drizzle on the oil. Cover with a lid.
2. Microwave at power level LOW & DEFROST for 40 to 48 minutes, or until peppers are very soft, stirring occasionally. Serve hot, at room temperature, or chilled.

Makes 4 to 6 servings.

SAUSAGE-STUFFED ONIONS

3 large yellow onions
⅛ cup water

¼ pound pork sausage, crumbled, casings removed
¼ cup shredded Swiss cheese
¼ cup grated Parmesan cheese
1 tablespoon finely chopped parsley
⅛ teaspoon salt
⅛ teaspoon pepper

3 tablespoons bread crumbs
1 tablespoon butter or margarine, cut into 3 slices

1. Peel onions and cut ½ inch off the sprout ends. Cut off just enough of the root ends so that the onions will sit flat. Arrange onions in a 10-inch round baking dish. Pour water into the dish and cover loosely with a sheet of wax paper. Microwave at power level HIGH for 10 to 15 minutes, or until onions are crisp-tender with pierced with a fork. Remover the centers of the onions as they pop up during cooking.
2. Carefully scrape out the centers of the onions, leaving a ½-inch shell. Chop removed onion centers coarsely and combine in a 1-quart glass casserole with the sausage. Microwave onion-sausage mixture, uncovered, at power level HIGH for 4 minutes, or until sausage is lightly browned, stirring twice. Drain off fat. Stir in cheese, parsley, salt, and pepper. Stuff onions with sausage mixture.
3. Sprinkle each onion with 1 tablespoon bread crumbs and top with a pat of butter. Microwave, covered with wax paper, at power level HIGH for 5 to 7 minutes, or until heated through. Let stand, covered, 5 minutes before serving.

Makes 3 servings.

ORANGE BEETS

1 16-ounce can beets, drained, ½ cup liquid reserved
1 tablespoon cornstarch
½ cup orange juice
2 tablespoons honey
1 teaspoon grated orange peel
¼ teaspoon ground ginger
big pinch grated nutmeg
1 11-ounce can mandarin oranges, drained

1. Place cornstarch in a 1½-quart glass casserole. Stir in beet liquid and orange juice. Add all remaining ingredients, except beets, and stir to blend. Microwave, uncovered, at power level HIGH for 4 to 5 minutes, or until hot and thickened, stirring twice.
2. Add beets to sauce mixture. Microwave, uncovered, at power level HIGH for 3 to 4 minutes, or until beets are warmed through, stirring once. Gently stir in the oranges.
Let stand 3 minutes before serving.

Makes 4 servings.

CREOLE-STYLE OKRA

½ cup sliced onion
4 tablespoons butter or margarine

2 10-ounce packages frozen okra
1 16-ounce can stewed tomatoes, broken up
1 teaspoon Worcestershire sauce
¼ teaspoon hot pepper sauce
½ teaspoon salt
¼ teaspoon pepper

1. Combine onion and butter in a 2-quart glass casserole. Microwave, uncovered, at power level HIGH for 5 to 6 minutes, or until onion if fairly tender, stiring twice.
2. Add all remaining ingredients. Cover. Microwave at power level HIGH for 15 to 19 minutes, or until okra is tender, stirring 3 times. Let stand, covered, 3 to 5 minutes before serving.

Makes 6 servings.

PASTA, RICE & CEREAL

Lasagna
(Recipe on page 67)

BASIC COOKING OF PASTA

2 quarts water
2 tablespoons salt
2 tablespoons oil
½ pound pasta break in half.

1. Combine water, salt, and oil in a 3-quart glass casserole. Microwave, uncovered, at power level HIGH for 10 to 13 minutes, or until boiling. To cook long pasta shapes, such as spaghetti and lasagna noodles, place pasta in a 10-inch round baking dish and pour boiling water over it. To cook other pasta, simply add it to the casserole containing boiling water.
2. Microwave, uncovered, at power level HIGH according to the times indicated in the chart below, stirring twice. Let stand 3 minutes. Drain.

Makes 4 servings.

pasta, 8 ounces	Approximate cooking time	Standing time
egg noodles, medium width	6 to 7½ minutes	3 minutes.
elbow macaroni	9 to 10 minutes	3 minutes.
bows, shells, spirals	13 to 15 minutes	3 minutes.
spaghetti, medium thickness	8 to 10 minutes	3 minutes.
lasagna noodles	15 to 19 minutes	3 minutes.

FETTUCCINE ALFREDO

8 tablespoons (1 stick) butter, cut into
1-tablespoon pieces
½ cup whipping cream

½ pound medium-width egg noodles, cooked according to chart on page 65
1 cup grated Parmesan cheese
¼ to ½ teaspoon pepper, preferably freshly ground

1. Combine butter and cream in a 1½-quart glass mixing bowl or microwave-safe serving bowl. Microwave, uncovered, at power level HIGH for 4 to 5 minutes, or until mixture boils, stirring twice.
2. Stir hot cooked, drained noodles into butter-cream mixture. Toss. Add Parmesan cheese and toss again. Sprinkle on pepper and toss. Serve at once.

Makes 4 servings.

NOODLES FLORENTINE

½ pound medium-width egg noodles, cooked according to chart on page 65
1 10-ounce package frozen chopped spinach, thawed and well drained
2 cups shredded Swiss cheese
1 8-ounce container sour cream
½ cup whipping cream
¼ cup finely chopped green onion
⅛ teaspoon ground nutmeg
½ teaspoon salt
¼ teaspoon pepper

1. Combine all ingredients in a 2-quart glass casserole. Blend well. Cover.
2. Microwave at power level HIGH for about 13½ minutes, or until heated through, stirring 3 times. Let stand, covered, 3 minutes before serving.

Makes 6 servings.

RICE PILAF

1 cup long grain rice
6 tablespoons butter or margarine
¼ cup finely chopped onion
¼ cup finely chopped celery

2¼ cups chicken broth
1 small bay leaf
⅛ teaspoon ground thyme
¼ teaspoon salt
¼ teaspoon pepper

1. Combine rice and butter in a 2-quart glass casserole Microwave, uncovered, at power level HIGH for 4 to 5 minutes, or until rice has begun to brown, stirring every minute. Add onion and celery. Microwave, uncovered, at power level HIGH for 2½ to 4 minutes longer, or until vegetables are softened.
2. Stir in all remaining ingredients. Cover. Set microwave oven at power level HIGH for 6 minutes, and then power level LOW & DEFROST for 15 minutes. Stir twice during cooking. Let rice stand, covered, 5 minutes before serving.

Makes 6 servings.

RICE WITH PEAS

½ cup finely chopped onion
½ cup finely chopped mushrooms
4 tablespoons butter or margarine

1 cup long-grain rice
2 cups chicken broth
1 10-ounce package frozen peas, thawed
¼ teaspoon salt
¼ teaspoon pepper

1. Combine onions, mushrooms, and butter in a 2-quart glass casserole. Microwave, uncovered, at power level HIGH for 5 to 6 minutes, or until vegetables are softened, stirring twice.
2. Add all remaining ingredients. Set microwave oven at power level HIGH for 6 minutes, and then power level LOW & DEFROST for 18 minutes. Stir 3 times during cooking. Let stand, covered, 5 minutes before serving.

Makes 6 servings.

MICROWAVING QUICK-COOKING CEREALS

⅓ cup cereal
¾ cup water
⅛ teaspoon salt

1. Measure ⅓ cup cereal, ¾ cup water, and ⅛ teaspoon salt into each individual serving bowl. Mix well.
2. Microwave, uncovered, at power level HIGH according to the times indicated in the chart below. Stir. Let stand 1 to 2 minutes before serving.

servings	approximate cooking time
1	1 to 1½ minutes
2	1½ to 2 minutes
4	3½ to 4 minutes

FRUITY OATMEAL

4 cups hot water
2 cups quick-cooking oats
⅔ cup chopped dried apricots or raisins
¼ cup packed dark brown sugar
¼ teaspoon salt

1 tablespoon butter
1 teaspoon ground cinnamon
⅛ teaspoon ground nutmeg
⅛ teaspoon ground ginger
dash ground cloves or allspice

1. Combine water, oats, fruit, sugar, and salt in a 2-quart casserole. Cover. Microwave at power level HIGH for 5 to 6 minutes, or until oatmeal bubbles and thickens, stirring twice.
2. Add all remaining ingredients and stir to blend. Cover and let stand 3 minutes before serving.

Makes 4 servings.

MACARONI AND CHEESE

½ pound uncooked elbow macaroni
2 cups hot water
6 tablespoons butter or margarine
½ cup finely chopped onion
¾ teaspoon salt
¼ teaspoon pepper

2¼ cups milk
12 ounces process American cheese, cut into
    cubes (about 3 cups)
⅓ cup flour

1. Combine macaroni, water, butter, onion, salt, and pepper in a 2-quart casserole. Cover. Set microwave oven at power level HIGH for 6 minutes, and then power level LOW & DEFROST for 8 minutes. Stir twice during cooking.
2. Stir in remaining ingredients. Cover. Microwave at power level HIGH for 15 to 19 minutes, or until macaroni is tender and sauce is thickened and bubbly, stirring every 3 minutes.

Makes 4 servings.

LASAGNA

½ pound ground beef
½ pound sausage meat
1 8-ounce can tomato sauce
1 4-ounce can mushroom pieces, drained
1 teaspoon oregano or basil
1 clove-garlic, pressed or finely chopped
½ teaspoon salt
¼ teaspoon pepper

¼ pound lasagna noodles, cooked
    according to chart on page 65
1 6-ounce carton cream-style cottage
    cheese or ricotta
½ 6-ounce package sliced mozzarella cheese
⅓ cup grated Parmesan cheese

1. Crumble beef and sausage into a 1-quart glass casserole. Cover. Microwave at power level HIGH for 5 to 8 minutes, or until meat is lightly browned, stirring 3 times. Drain off fat. Stir in tomato sauce, mushrooms, oregano, garlic, salt, and pepper.
2. In a 2-quart casserole, layer ⅓ of the noodles and top with ⅓ of the sauce and ½ of the cottage cheese and mozzarella cheese. Add a second layer of ⅓ of the noodles, ⅓ of the sauce, and the remainder of the cottage cheese and mozzarella cheese. Cover with last ⅓ of the noodles and last ⅓ of the sauce. Sprinkle with Parmesan cheese. Cover. Microwave at power level HIGH for 15 to 17 minutes, or until lasagna is hot at the center. Let stand, covered, 5 minutes before serving.

Makes 3 to 4 servings.

GREAT GRANOLA

1½ cups oats, either quick-cooking or
    old-fashioned
½ cup coarsely chopped nuts, preferably
    almonds and/or filberts
¼ cup wheat germ
¼ cup packed dark brown sugar
⅛ cup honey
1 teaspoon vanilla extract

¼ cup shredded coconut
¼ cup chopped apricots
¼ cup raisins

1. Place oats in a 10-inch round baking dish. Microwave at power level HIGH for 3 minutes, stirring twice. Mix in nuts, wheat germ, and brown sugar. Stir in honey and vanilla. Microwave, uncovered, at power level HIGH for 3 to 5 minutes, stirring 2 times.
2. Add coconut, apricots, and raisins to cereal mixture. Stir occasionally as granola cools to break up. Store in a tightly lidded container.

Makes about 3 cups.

EGGS & CHEESE

Spinach Ring with Cheese
(Recipe on page 70)

BASIC SCRAMBLED EGGS

1. Use a 10-ounce bowl or custard cup for 1 to 2 egg; use a 1-quart bowl for 4 to 6 eggs. Beat eggs and milk together with a fork until well blended. Cut butter into small pieces and stir into eggs.
2. Microwave, uncovered at power level HIGH according to the times given in the chart below. Break up and stir eggs with a fork every 30 seconds. Cook until nearly set, then let stand, covered loosely, for 1 to 3 minutes to complete cooking. Stir and season to taste with salt and pepper.

eggs	milk	butter	cooking time
1	1 tablespoon	1 teaspoon	¾ to 1¼ minutes.
2	2 tablespoons	2 teaspoons	1¾ to 2¼ minutes.
4	¼ cup	4 teaspoons	3 to 2½ minutes.
6	⅓ cup	2 tablespoons	4 to 5 minutes

BASIC OMELET

1 tablespoon butter or margarine

2 eggs
2 tablespoons milk
⅛ teaspoon salt
dash pepper
¼ cup shredded cheese or ¼ cup diced
ham or ¼ cup jelly (optional)

1. Place butter in a 9-inch glass pie plate. Microwave, uncovered, at power level HIGH for 30 seconds, or until melted. Tilt plate to cover bottom with melted butter.
2. Combine eggs, milk, salt, and pepper in a small bowl, beating to blend thoroughly. Pour mixture into pie plate. Microwave at power level HIGH for 2 to 2½ minutes, or until nearly set, stirirng once after 1 minute' cooking time. Let stand, covered, 2 minutes to set completely.
3. If desired, spread a filling such as shredded cheese, diced ham, or jelly on top of the omelet. Fold in thirds like a business letter.

Makes 1 to 2 servings.

BASIC POACHED EGGS

1. Combine 1 cup water and ½ teaspoon vinegar in a 1-quart glass casserole. Microwave, uncovered, at power level HIGH for 4 minutes, or until water boils.
2. Carefully break eggs into water one at a time, pushing them to the center of the casserole with the back of a spoon. Cover with wax paper. Microwave at power level HIGH according to the times given in the chart below. Let stand, covered, 1½ to 2 minutes before serving.

eggs	cooking time
1	1 minute and 30 seconds
2	1 minute and 45 seconds
4	2 minutes and 30 seconds

EGGS BENEDICT

1 1¼-ounce package Hollandaise sauce
  mix, prepared and heated according to
  package directions
4 eggs, poached according to recipe on
  page 69
2 English muffins, split and toasted
4 thin slices cooked ham

1. Have Hollandaise sauce, poached eggs, and English muffins ready. Place ham slices in a single layer on a paper plate lined with a paper towel. Microwave at power level HIGH for 1 to 1½ minutes, or until heated through.
2. Place English muffin halves on a platter or on individual plates. Cover each with a slice of ham and top with a poached egg. Spoon sauce on top. If necessary, reheat by microwaving, uncovered, at power level HIGH for ½ to 1 minute.

Makes 2 to 4 servings.

SHRIMP SCRAMBLED EGGS

8 eggs
1 11-ounce can condensed cream of shrimp
   soup
1 4½-ounce can mushrooms pieces, drained
1 3½-ounce can shrimp, drained
2 tablespoons chopped green onion
1 tablespoon dried parsley flakes
¼ teaspoon salt
¼ teaspoon pepper

1. Combine all ingredients in a 2-quart glass casserole and beat to blend well.
2. Microwave, uncovered, at power level HIGH for 6 to 7 minutes, or until nearly set, breaking up eggs with a fork and stirring every minute. Stir at the end of cooking time, then let stand 2 to 3 minutes before serving.

Makes 4 to 6 servings.

GIANT BROCCOLI OMELET

1 10-ounce package frozen chopped
   broccoli
4 eggs
¼ cup shredded Cheddar cheese
⅛ cup finely chopped onion
1 tablespoon milk
⅛ teaspoon tarragon (optional)
small pinch ground nutmeg
½ teaspoon salt
⅛ teaspoon pepper

1. Place broccoli in a 9-inch round baking dish. Cover. Microwave at power level HIGH for 5 to 6 minutes, or until broccoli is crisp-tender, stirring once. Drain thoroughly.
2. Beat all remaining ingredients together in a 1½-quart mixing bowl, then pour mixture over broccoli. Elevate baking dish in the oven by placing it on an inverted dinner plate. Cover with wax paper. Microwave at power level HIGH for 6 to 7 minutes, or until center is almost set, stirring once with a fork after 3½ minutes.
Let stand, covered, 3 to 5 minutes before serving.

Makes 2 to 3 servings.

SPINACH RING WITH CHEESE

2 10-ounce packages frozen chopped
   spinach, thawed and well drained
1 cup cottage cheese
½ cup shredded Swiss cheese
¼ cup grated Parmesan cheese
2 eggs
½ teaspoon ground thyme
½ teaspoon salt
¼ teaspoon pepper
¼ cup buttered bread crumbs (optional)

1. Combine all ingredients, except buttered crumbs, in a 2-quart mixing bowl. Blend thoroughly. Pour mixture into a well-buttered microwave-safe 6-to 8-cup ring mold. Cover with wax paper.
2. Microwave at power level HIGH for 9 to 10½ minutes, or until mold is set. Let stand, covered, 5 minutes. Turn out onto serving platter. Sprinkle, if desired, with buttered crumbs, and fill with scrambled eggs or a creamed food.

Makes 6 to 8 servings.

EGGS AND HASH BROWN POTATOES

¼ cup chopped green pepper
¼ cup chopped onion
2 tablespoons oil
1 12-ounce package frozen hash brown
   potatoes
1½ cups cut-up cooked ham

4 eggs
⅛ teaspoon pepper

1. Combine green pepper, onion, and oil in a 2-quart glass casserole. Microwave, uncovered, at power level HIGH for 6 minutes, stirring twice. Add potatoes. Cover and microwave at power level HIGH for 9 minutes, or until partially cooked, breaking up twice. Add ham, cover, and microwave at power level HIGH for 4½ to 6 minutes, or until mixture is heated, stirring twice.
2. Make 4 hollows in the potato mixture all around the edge of the dish and break the eggs into the indentations. Pierce the yolks twice and the whites 3 times with a toothpick. Sprinkle eggs with pepper. Cover with a lid. Microwave at power level HIGH for 3½ to 5½ minutes, or until eggs are done to taste. Let stand, covered, 2 minutes before serving.

Makes 4 servings.

RANCHERO EGGS

¼ cup oil
¼ cup finely chopped green pepper
¼ cup finely chopped onion
I clove garlic, pressed or finely chopped
1 28-ounce can tomatoes
1 3-ounce can chilies, drained and mashed
¾ teaspoon salt
½ teaspoon pepper

6 eggs
1 cup Monterey jack or Cheddar cheese

1. Combine oil, green pepper, onion, and garlic in a 9-inch round baking dish. Microwave, uncovered, at power level HIGH for 6 minutes, or until vegetables are fairly tender, stirring twice. Stir in tomatoes, mashing with a fork to break up, along with chilies, salt, and pepper. Cover and microwave at power level HIGH for 6 minutes, stirring once.
2. Break eggs into the tomato mixture along the edge of the dish. Using a toothpick, pierce each egg yolk twice and each white 3 times. Cover. Microwave at power level HIGH for 5½ to 8 minutes, or until eggs are done to taste. Sprinkle with cheese, cover, and let stand 5 minutes before serving.

Makes 3 to 6 servings.

CHEESE SOUFFLE

⅓ cup flour
1½ cups milk
½ teaspoon salt
½ teaspoon pepper, preferably white pepper

1 cup shredded Swiss cheese
½ cup greated Parmesan cheese
2 tablespoons butter or margarine, cut into pats
6 eggs, separated

½ teaspoon cream of tartar

1. Place flour in a 4-cup glass measure. Slowly add milk, beating to make a smooth paste. Stir in salt and pepper. Microwave, uncovered, at power level HIGH for 4 to 6 minutes, or until mixture thickens and come to a boil, stirring every minute.
2. Add cheese and butter to milk mixture. Stir until butter melts completely and cheese melts partially, about 1 minute. Stir in 6 egg yolks.
3. Beat egg whites with cream of tartar in a grease-free 2-quart glass or metal mixing bowl until moist but stiff peaks form. Gently pour cheese mixture onto whites. Fold delicately with a plastic spatula until whites and cheese sauce are fairly well blended. Pour into u ngreased 2-quart glass casserole or souffle dish.
4. Microwave, uncovered, at power level LOW & DEFROST for 38 to 45 minutes, or until set. Serve at once.

Makes 4 to 6 servings.

WELSH RAREBIT

4 tablespoons butter or margarine
¼ cup flour
½ teaspoon dry mustard
½ teaspoon Worcestershire sauce
big pinch cayenne pepper
big pinch ground nutmeg
½ teaspoon salt
¼ teaspoon pepper
1 cup milk

½ cup beer, cider, or white wine
2 cups shredded Cheddar cheese
toast, biscuits, or toasted English muffins

1. Place butter in a 1½-quart glass casserole. Microwave at power level HIGH for 1½ to 2½ minutes, or until melted. Stir in flour and seasonings, blending to make a smooth plaste. Add milk, stirring until smooth. Microwave, uncovered, at power level HIGH for 4 minutes, or until boiling and thickened, stirring every minute. Mixture will be very thick.
2. Stir beer into milk mixture. Add cheese. Microwave, uncovered, at power level HIGH for 3½ to 4½ minutes, or until cheese has melted, stirring every minute. Serve over toast, biscuits, or toasted English muffins.

Makes 3 to 4 servings.

Ranchero Eggs
(Recipe on page 71)

SALMON FONDUE

1 8-ounce package cream cheese
1 5-ounce jar sharp process cheese spread
3 tablespoons milk
1 small clove garlic, pressed or finely
   chopped
½ teaspoon Worcestershire sauce
big pinch cayenne pepper

1 7-ounce can salmon or tuna, drained and
   flaked
toasted cubes of French bread

1. Combine all ingredients, except fish and bread, in a 1½-quart glass bowl. Microwave, uncovered, at power level LOW & DEFROST for 4½ to 8 minutes, or until cream cheese is soft. Stir to blend thoroughly. Microwave, uncovered, at power level HIGH for 2½ minutes, stirring once.
2. Add salmon or tuna to cheese mixture. Microwave, uncovered, at power level HIGH for 2½ to 4 minutes, or until heated through, stirring once. Use French bread cubes for dipping into the fondue.

Makes about 2½ cups.

Notes

SANDWICHES

Pizza Rolls
(Recipe on page 75)

BEAN DOGS

1 8-ounce can pork and beans in molasses
  sauce
3 slices bacon, cooked and crumbled
1 tablespoon prepared mustard
¼ teaspoon chili powder

4 frankfurters
4 frankfurter rolls

1. Combine all ingredients, except frankfurters and rolls, in a 1-quart mixing bowl. Stir briskly so that beans become slightly mashed.
2. Arrange frankfurters in rolls and top with bean mixture. Wrap each frankfurter loosely in a paper towel or napkin. Place on a baking tray. Microwave at power level HIGH for 6 to 8 minutes, or until heated through.

Makes 4 servings.

CHEESEBURGERS

1 pound ground beef

4 slices American process cheese
4 hamburger rolls

1. Shape ground beef into 4 4-inch patties. Arrange in a baking dish. Microwave, uncovered, at power level HIGH for 3 to 5 minutes, or until done to taste, turning patties over and draining liquid once.
2. Top patties with slices of cheese. Cover and microwave at power level HIGH for 1 minute. Let stand, covered, 2 minutes before serving on hamburger rolls.

Makes 4 servings.

PIZZA ROLLS

1 pound ground beef
¼ cup finely chopped onion
1 clove garlic, pressed or finely chopped
½ cup thick tomato sauce
½ teaspoon basil or oregano
½ teaspoon salt
½ teaspoon pepper

2 Italian rolls (about 6 inches long each)
¾ cup shredded mozzarella cheese

1. Combine beef, onion, and garlic in a 1-quart glass baking dish. Cover. Microwave at power level HIGH for 7½ to 9 minutes, or until beef begins to brown, stirring twice. Drain off fat.
Stir in tomato sauce, oregano, salt, and pepper.
2. Split rolls in half lengthwise and arrange in a round baking dish. Spoon on beef mixture and top with cheese. Microwave, uncovered, at power level LOW & DEFROST for 11 to 12½ minutes, or until the cheese is melted and sandwiches are hot.

Makes 4 servings.

SLOPPY JOES

1 pound ground beef
½ cup finely chopped onion
½ cup finely chopped celery
½ cup finely chopped green pepper

1 cup tomato sauce
1 tablespoon packed dark brown sugar
pinch ground thyme
½ teaspoon salt
¼ teaspoon pepper
4 hamburger rolls, split

1. Crumble beef into a 2-quart glass casserole. Combine beef with onion, celery, and green pepper. Cover. Microwave at power level HIGH for 7½ to 9 minutes, or until beef is browned, stirring 3 times. Drain.
2. Add all remaining ingredients. Cover. Set microwave oven at power level HIGH for 4 minutes, and then power level LOW & DEFROST for 19 minutes. Stir twice during cooking. Let stand, covered, 3 minutes before serving on hamburger rolls.

Makes 4 servings.

BARBECUED BEEF SANDWICHES

8 slices rye bread or 4 hard rolls, cut in half lengthwise
1 pound sliced cooked roast beef
½ cup barbecue or chili sauce
4 thin slices onion (optional)
1 medium dill pickle, thinly sliced (optional)

1. Arrange 4 slices rye bread or the bottom slices of 4 hard rolls on a glass oven tray. Top with half the roast beef slices and spread with chili sauce. Place optional onion and pickle slices over chili sauce, cover with remaining roast beef, and close sandwiches with 4 bread slices or hard roll tops. Wrap sandwiches individually in paper towels or napkins.
2. Microwave at power level LOW & DEFROST for 4½ to 6½ minutes, or until heated through. Let stand 1 minutes before serving.

Makes 4 servings.

REUBEN SANDWICHES

4 slices dark rye or pumpernickel bread
½ pound thinly sliced, cooked, corned beef
½ cup creamy Russian or Thousand Island dressing
1 8-ounce can sauerkraut, rinsed and well drained
4 rectangular slices Swiss cheese, folded over to fit sandwiches

1. Place bread on a baking tray lined with paper toweling. Top with corned beef. Spread dressing over corned beef. Cover with sauerkraut and place cheese on top.
2. Microwave, uncovered, at power level LOW & DEFROST for 6½ to 8 minutes, or until sandwich is heated through and cheese has melted.

Makes 4 servings.

OPEN-FACED FRIJOLE SANDWICHES

1 8-ounce can refried beans
1 3-ounce can green chilies, drained and mashed
¼ cup finely chopped onion
¼ cup finely chopped green pepper
1 clove garlic, pressed or finely chopped (optional)
¼ to ½ teaspoon salt
4 slices white bread, toasted

1 to 1½ cups shredded Cheddar cheese
½ cup cubed tomatoes
1 cup finely shredded lettuce

1. Combine beans, chilies, onion, green pepper, garlic, and salt in a small bowl and blend well. Spread mixture evenly on toast slices. Arrange open-faces on a glass baking tray and cover loosely with wax paper. Microwave at power level LOW & DEFROST for 8 to 9½ minutes, or until heated.
2. Sprinkle Cheddar cheese on top of open-faces. Microwave, uncovered, at power level HIGH for 1 to 2 minutes, or until cheese melts. Remove sandwiches to serving platter or individual plates. Top with cubed tomatoes and shredded lettuce.

Makes 4 servings.

HAM AND EGG SANDWICHES

¼ cup finely chopped onion
¼ cup finely chopped green pepper
3 tablespoons butter or margarine

4 eggs, lightly beaten
⅓ to ⅔ cup cubed cooked ham
1 small tomato, seeded and well drained

4 hamburger rolls or hard rolls

1. Combine onion, green pepper, and butter in a 9-inch round baking dish. Microwave, uncovered, at power level HIGH for 6 minutes, stirring twice.
2. Add remaining ingredients, except rolls, to baking dish. Microwave, uncovered, at power level HIGH for 4 to 4½ minutes, or until nearly firm, stirring and breaking up the mixture once after 2½ minutes' cooking time. Let stand 2 to 3 minutes before serving to allow to set completely. Cut into wedges and place on rolls. If desired, spread with mayonnaise and top with lettuce.

Makes 4 servings.

HOT TUNA SANDWICHES

1 7-ounce can tuna, drained
½ cup mayonnaise
2 tablespoons finely chopped onion
2 tablespoons finely chopped celery
2 tablespoons finely chopped green pepper
¼ teaspoon Worcestershire sauce
¼ teaspoon salt
¼ teaspoon pepper
4 hamburger rolls or hard rolls
4 slices American process cheese

1. Combine all ingredients, except rolls and cheese slices, and blend well in a 1-quart bowl. Spread tuna mixture on the 4 bottom slices of the rolls. Top with a slice of cheese and close sandwiches with top slices of rolls. Wrap sandwiches individually in paper towels or napkins and arrange on an oven tray.
2. Microwave at power level HIGH for 3½ to 5½ minutes, or until sandwiches are warmed and cheese has begun to melt.
Let stand 1 to 2 minutes before serving.

Makes 4 servings.

MIDDLE EAST SANDWICHES

1 cup plain yoghurt
½ cup chopped green pepper
2 tablespoons finely chopped onion
¼ teaspoon dried mint

1½ pounds ground beef
2 cloves garlic, pressed or finely chopped
1 8-ounce can stewed tomatoes, chopped
1 tablespoon dried parsley flakes

4 individual loaves Middle Eastern pocket (pita) bread
1½ cups shredded lettuce

1. Mix together yoghurt, green pepper, onion, and mint in a small bowl. Set aside.
2. Combine beef and garlic in a 2-quart glass casserole. Cover. Microwave at power level HIGH for 7½ to 9 minutes, or until beef begins to brown, stirring twice. Drain off fat. Stir in tomatoes and parsley flakes. Cover. Microwave at power level HIGH for 6 to 7½ minutes, or until hot, stirring once.
3. Cut a 1½-inch piece off each loaf of bread. Gently open the pocket of the larger remaining piece of the loaf. Fill pocket with beef mixture and top with shredded lettuce and yoghurt dressing.

Makes 4 servings.

Notes

BREADS

Apricot Walnut Bread
(Recipe on page 79)

BANANA BREAD

2 cups packaged biscuit mix
½ cup packed dark brown sugar
3 tablespoons flour
¼ teaspoon ground nutmeg or mace
¼ teaspoon salt
¼ cup milk
1 egg, lightly beaten
⅔ cup mashed banana
⅔ cup snipped dates
⅔ cup chopped walnuts

1. Combine biscuit mix, brown sugar, flour, spices, and salt in a midium mixing bowl and stir to blend. Combine milk, egg, and banana in glass measure and add to dry mixture, stirring only until all ingredients are moistened. Stir in dates and nuts. Pour batter into a wellgreased glass loaf dish. Do not cover. Place dish on an inverted saucer or cereal bowl in the oven.

2. Set microwave oven at power level LOW & DEFROST for 19 minutes, and then power level HIGH for 5 minutes. If necessary, microwave an additional 3 to 8 minutes at power level HIGH to complete baking. Let loaf stand 10 minutes before removing from dish. Let stand an additional 5 minutes before serving.

Makes 1 loaf.

APRICOT WALNUT BREAD

¼ cup milk
½ cup water
1 cup chopped dried apricots
grated peel or 1 orange

¾ cup packed dark brown sugar
1 egg, lightly beaten
3 tablespoons oil
¾ cup chopped walnuts
1½ cups flour
1 teaspoon baking powder
¼ teaspoon ground nutmeg or mace
½ teaspoon salt

1. Combine milk, water, dried apricots, and orange peel in a 2-quart glass bowl. Microwave, uncovered, at power level HIGH for 2½ to 4 minutes, or until mixture boils, stirring once.

2. Add brown sugar, egg, and oil to fruit mixture, beating to blend well. Stir in remaining ingredients, Pour batter into a well-greased loaf dish. Do not cover. Place dish on an inverted saucer or cereal bowl in the oven to elevate.

3. Set microwave oven at power level LOW & DEFROST for 16 minutes, and then power level HIGH for 4 minutes. If necessary, microwave at power level HIGH an additional 4 to 9 minutes to complete baking. Let loaf stand 10 minutes before removing from dish. Let stand an additional 5 minutes before serving.

Makes 1 loaf.

PUMPKIN BREAD

1 cup canned pumpkin
2 eggs
1 teaspoon vanilla
1 cup chopped walnuts or pecans
½ cup oil
⅓ cup water
½ teaspoon ground cinnamon
½ teaspoon ground cloves or allspice
½ teaspoon ground nutmeg or mace
1½ cups sugar
1¼ cups flour
1 teaspoon baking soda
½ teaspoon salt

1. In a 1-quart mixing bowl, combine pumpkin, eggs, vanilla, nuts, oil, water, and spices. Stir in sugar. Combine flour, baking soda, and salt in a separate bowl, then stir into pumpkin mixture. Blend only until all ingredients are moistened. Turn batter into a well-greased glass loaf dish. Do not cover. Place dish on an inverted saucer or cereal bowl in the oven to elevate.

2. Set microwave oven at power level LOW & DEFROST for 19 minutes, and then power level HIGH for 7½ minutes. If necessary, microwave at power level HIGH an additional 4 to 9 minutes to complete baking. Let loaf stand 10 minutes before removing from dish. Let stand an additional 5 minutes before serving.

Makes 1 loaf.

Orange Coffe Cake Ring
(Recipe on page 82)

CARAWAY BREAD

3 cups flour
3 tablespoons sugar
¾ teaspoon baking powder
1 teaspoon salt
3 tablespoons butter or margarine
1½ cups raisins
1 tablespoon caraway seeds
1 tablespoon grated orange peel
1 cup buttermilk
1 egg
1 teaspoon baking soda

1. In a 2-quart mixing bowl, stir together flour, sugar, baking powder, and salt. Cut in butter. Stir in raisins, caraway seeds, and orange peel. Beat buttermilk, egg, and baking soda to blend in a small bowl. Stir liquid mixture into dry ingredients, blending only until dry ingredients are moistened.
2. On a lightly floured surface, quickly and lightly knead the dough, just until smooth, about 1 to 2 minutes. Shape into a ball and cut a cross in the top of the dough about ½ inch deep. Line a 1-quart glass bowl with wax paper. Place dough inside bowl. Do not cover.
3. Microwave at power level HIGH for 10 to 11½ minutes, or until dough is firm. Let stand 10 minutes before turning out of bowl. Let stand an additional 10 minutes before serving.

Makes 1 round loaf.

CORN MUFFINS

½ cup flour
½ cup yellow corn meal
2 tablespoons sugar
2 teaspoons baking powder
¼ teaspoon baking soda
¼ teaspoon salt
1 egg, lightly beaten
½ cup milk or buttermilk
2 tablespoons oil or melted butter

1. In a 1½-quart mixing bowl, combine flour, corn meal, sugar, baking powder, baking soda and salt. Add egg, milk, and oil and stir just until all ingredients are moistened. Spoon batter into 8 6-ounce custard cups lined with cupcake papers.
2. Arrange 4 custard cups on a round baking tray. Microwave, uncovered, at power level HIGH for 2½ to 4 minutes. Repeat procedure with remaining 4 custard cups. Let muffins stand 3 minutes before serving.

Makes 8 muffins.

BRAN MUFFINS

⅓ cup milk
1 egg
½ cup whole bran cereal
¼ cup oil
¼ cup raisins
¼ cup molasses
¾ cup flour
1 teaspoon baking powder
¼ teaspoon baking soda
¼ teaspoon ground cinnamon
¼ teaspoon salt

1. Beat milk and egg together in a 1½-quart mixing bowl. Stir in bran cereal and let stand 1 minute. Stir in oil, raisins, and molasses. Add flour, baking powder, baking soda, cinnamon, and salt, stirring only until all ingredients are moistened. Spoon batter into 8 6-ounce custard cups lined with cupcake papers.
2. Arrange 4 custard cups on a round baking tray. Microwave, uncovered, at power level HIGH for 2½ to 4 minutes. Repeat procedure with remaining 4 custard cups. Let muffins stand 3 minutes before serving.

Makes 8 muffins.

PINEAPPLE MUFFINS

1 8-ounce can crushed pineapple, well drained, ¼ cup syrup reserved
⅓ cup packed dark brown sugar
3 tablespoons butter or margarine
1 egg
1 cup flour
½ cup chopped pecans or walnuts
1 teaspoon baking powder
½ teaspoon salt

1. In a 1½-quart mixing bowl, cream together drained pineapple, brown sugar, and butter. Beat in egg and reserved syrup. Add flour, nuts, baking powder, and salt, stirring only until dry ingredients are moistened. Turn batter into 8 6-ounce custard cups lined with cupcake papers.
2. Arrange 4 custard cups on a round baking tray. Microwave, uncovered, at power level HIGH for 2½ to 4 minutes. Repeat procedure with remaining 4 custard cups. Let muffins stand 5 minutes before serving.

Makes 8 muffins.

STICKY BUNS

5 tablespoons butter or margarine
5 tablespoons packed dark brown sugar
5 tablespoons chopped pecans or walnuts
¼ teaspoon ground cinnamon

⅔ cup buttermilk baking mix
¼ cup cold water
⅔ tablespoon grated orange peel

1. Place 5 6-ounce custard cups in a circle on a baking tray. In each cup, place 1 tablespoon butter. Microwave, uncovered, at power level HIGH for 2½ to 4 minutes, or until butter has melted. Swirl custard cups to coat the sides with butter. Add one tablespoon each brown sugar and chopped nuts to each cup. Dust with cinnamon. Return to oven and microwave, uncovered, at power level HIGH for about 4 minutes, or until hot and bubbly.
2. Blend remaining ingredients together in a small mixing bowl, beating only until smooth. Spoon batter evenly into custard cups. Microwave, uncovered, at power level HIGH for 4 to 5 minutes, or until tops spring back when pressed with a finger. Immediately invert custard cups onto a serving platter. Allow buns to rest, covered with custard cups, for 2 minutes before serving.

Makes 5 large buns.

ORANGE COFFEE CAKE RING

1 tablespoon butter or margarine, softened
¼ cup finely chopped walnuts or pecans
2 tablespoons packed dark brown sugar

¼ cup sugar
½ cup orange juice
1 egg
2 cups buttermilk baking mix
½ cup finely chopped walnuts
½ cup orange marmalade

1. Grease a 10-cup microwave-safe ring mold with softened butter and coat with nuts and brown sugar. Set aside.
2. Combine sugar, orange juice, and egg in a 1½-quart mixing bowl. Stir in baking mix to blend. Add walnuts and marmalade and stir only until all ingredients are mixed. Pour batter into prepared mold. Do not cover.
3. Set microwave oven at power level LOW & DEFROST for 9½ minutes, and then power level HIGH for 2½ minutes. If necessary, microwave at power level an additional 1½ to 6 minutes, to complete baking.
Let stand 5 minutes before inverting onto serving plate.

Makes 4 to 6 servings.

GARDEN YEAST BREAD

⅔ cup shredded carrot
⅔ cup chopped celery
⅓ cup water

3 cups flour
2 packages active dry yeast
2 teaspoons salt
¼ cup molasses
2 tablespoons oil
1 egg
1¼ cups warm water (but not hotter than 120°F)
½ cup wheat germ
¼ cup finely chopped parsley
1 to 2 tablespoons snipped chives or dried chives (optional)

1. Combine carrot, celery, and water in a 1-quart glass bowl. Cover. Microwave at power level HIGH for 6 minutes, stirring once. Drain well. Pat vegetables dry with paper toweling.
2. In a large mixer bowl, stir together 2 cups of the flour, yeast, and salt. Add molasses, oil, egg, and warm water. Beat with electric mixer at low speed for about 1 minute, or until blended, scraping down the sides of the bowl with a rubber spatula. Increase mixer speed to high and beat 3 minutes longer. Stir in carrot-celery mixture, remaining 1 cup flour, wheat germ, parsley, and chives. Knead 5 minutes, or till smooth.
3. Place a 4-cup measure containing 3 cups water in the oven and microwave at power level HIGH for 10 to 11½ minutes, or until boiling. Turn dough into a well-greased glass loaf pan and place it in the oven with the measure of hot water.
Microwave, uncovered, at power level LOW & DEFROST for 5 to 7 minutes, or until dough has risen nearly to double. Meanwhile, preheat conventional oven to 350°F.
4. Bake bread in preheated conventional oven for 50 to 60 minutes. If loaf browns too quickly, cover with aluminum foil. Remove from loaf pan when baked and let stand on a rack.

Makes 1 loaf.

GARLIC BREAD

8 tablespoons (1 stick) butter
1 to 1½ teaspoons garlic powder or 2 to 4 cloves garlic, pressed
¼ teaspoon salt
¼ teaspoon pepper, preferably freshly ground

1 14-inch loaf French bread, slashed ⅔ of the way through at 1-inch intervals

1. Combine butter, garlic, salt, and pepper in a 2-cup glass measure. Microwave, uncovered, at power level LOW & DEFROST for 1½ to 2 minutes, or until butter is softened, but not melted. Beat to blend.
2. Spread butter mixture between slashes in bread. Wrap loaf loosely in wax paper if a soft loaf is desired, but leave unwrapped for a slightly crisp loaf. Microwave at power level HIGH for 4 to 6 minutes, or until hot.

Makes 1 loaf.

Notes

CAKES & PIES

Coconut Cake
(Recipe on page 86)

DEVIL'S FOOD CAKE

¾ cup sugar
¼ cup butter or margarine, softened
1 egg
⅔ cup hot water
1 cup flour
¼ cup unsweetened cocoa
½ teaspoon vanilla extract
¾ teaspoon baking soda
½ teaspoon salt

1. In a 1-quart mixing bowl, cream together sugar and butter. Add egg, beating until fluffy. Blend in hot water. Stir in remaining ingredients, beating until thoroughly mixed.
2. Microwave at power level LOW & DEFROST for 16 to 20½ minutes, or until a toothpick inserted in the center comes out clean. Let stand 10 minutes before removing from dish.

Makes 1 layer.

SPICE CAKE

1½ cups sugar
½ cup butter or margarine, softened
1 egg
2¼ cups flour
2 teaspoons ground cinnamon
1 teaspoon ground nutmeg or mace
¾ teaspoon salt
¾ teaspoon baking powder
1½ cups buttermilk
1 cup raisins, tossed with 2 tablespoons
    flour

1. In a 3-quart mixing bowl, cream together sugar and butter until fluffy. Beat in egg. In a separate bowl, toss together flour, spices, salt, and baking powder. Add flour mixture and buttermilk alternately to sugar-butter mixture, beating until smooth. Toss raisins with flour and stir into batter.
2. Pour batter into a greased 10-cup bundt pan. Microwave, uncovered, at power level HIGH for 15 to 18 minutes, or until cake begins to pull away from the sides of the pan. Let stand, covered, 10 minutes before inverting onto a serving plate. If desired, drizzle with confectioners' sugar icing or sprinkle with confectioners' sugar.

Makes 1 cake.

PINEAPPLE UPSIDE-DOWN CAKE

2 tablespoons butter or margarine
1 9-ounce can pineapple tidbits, drained
1 tablespoon syrup reserved
¼ cup packed brown sugar

½ recipe butter cake

1. Place butter in 2-quart glass casserole and microwave, uncovered, at power level HIGH for 1½ to 2½ minutes, or until melted. Tilt dish to coat sides with butter. Stir 1 tablespoon reserved pineapple syrup and brown sugar into melted butter in the bottom of the dish. Arrange pineapple to cover bottom of dish.
2. Prepare butter cake. Gently ladle batter into prepared dish, being careful not to dishlodge pineapple. Microwave, uncovered, at power level HIGH for 10½ to 13½ minutes, or until toothpick inserted in the center comes out clean.
Let stand 2 minutes before inverting onto a serving platter.

Makes 4 servings.

FRUITCAKE

1 tablespoon butter
¼ cup graham cracker crumbs

8 ounces chopped dried apricots
 (about 2 cups)
8 ounces raisins or dried currants
 (about 1½ cups)
6 ounces slivered almonds (about 1½ cups)
1 cups candied cherries, halved
1 cup candied pineapple
¾ cup flour
¾ cup packed dark brown sugar
3 eggs
2 tablespoons rum or brandy
2 teaspoons vanilla extract
¼ teaspoon almond extract
½ teaspoon ground nutmeg or mace
½ teaspoon baking powder
½ teaspoon salt

1. Grease an 8-cup microwave-safe bundt pan with 1 tablespoon softened butter and coat with crumbs. Set aside.
2. Combine all remaining ingredients in a 3-quart mixing bowl. Blend well. Pour batter into prepared bundt pan. Microwave, uncovered, at power level LOW & DEFROST for 43 to 55 minutes, or until cake pulls away from the sides of the pan. Let stand 15 minutes on a counter before inverting onto a rack to cool. To store, wrap in foil or plastic and refrigerate for no longer than 4 weeks.

Makes 1 cake.

HONEY CAKE

3 eggs, separated
grated peel of 1 orange
grated peel of 1 lemon
½ cup honey
4 tablespoons melted butter or margarine
¾ cup flour
1 teaspoon ground cinnamon
1 teaspoon ground cloves or allspice
1 teaspoon ground nutmeg or mace
¾ teaspoon baking powder
½ teaspoon baking soda
⅛ teaspoon salt

1. In a very clean 2-quart bowl, beat egg whites until stiff peaks form. Set aside. In a separate 2-quart bowl, beat egg yolks and grated peels until yolks thicken slightly. Stir in honey and melted butter. Add flour, spices, baking powder and soda, and salt and beat until thoroughly blended. Fold in egg whites.
2. Pour batter into a well-greased loaf pan. Shield ends of the loaf with strips of aluminum foil. Place pan on an inverted saucer or cereal bowl in the oven to elevate. Microwave, uncovered, at power level LOW & DEFROST for 6½ minutes. Remove foil shields. Microwave at power level LOW & DEFROST an additional 3 to 9 minutes, or until top of the cake feels springy. Let stand on a counter for 5 minutes before inverting onto serving plate.

Makes 1 cake.

COCONUT CAKE

1 18½-ounce package yellow cake mix
1 3¾-ounce package coconut-flavored
 instant pudding mix
4 eggs
1 cup water
¼ cup oil
1 12-ounce jar strawberry or raspberry
 preserves
2 4½-ounce containers dessert topping,
 thawed
1½ cups flaked coconut

1. Combine cake mix, pudding mix, eggs, water, and oil in the large bowl of an electric mixer and beat at medium speed with mixer for 4 minutes. Pour batter into a well-greased 10 to 12-cup bundt pan. Microwave, uncovered at power level LOW & DEFROST for 22 to 27 minutes, or until there is no uncooked batter remaining near the bottom of the pan and the cake has begun to pull away from the sides of the pan. Let stand, covered, for 15 minutes before inverting onto a serving plate. Cover and let stand until cool.
2. Split cake horizontally into 3 layers Spread with preserves and reassemble. Frost with dessert topping and sprinkle with coconut. Store, covered, in the refrigerator until serving time.

Makes 1 cake.

APRICOT CHEESECAKE

1 16-ounce can apricot halves, drained
1 8-ounce package cream cheese, softened
⅓ cup sugar
2 eggs
1 tablespoon lemon juice
½ teaspoon vanilla extract

1 9-inch baked graham cracker crust
  (recipe on page 87)
additional apricot halves, if desired

1. Puree drained apricot halves in blender, food processor, or food mill. Combine with all remaining ingredients, except pie crust and additional apricot halves, and blend until smooth.
2. Pour mixture into prepared pie crust. Microwave, uncovered, at power level LOW & DEFROST for 22 to 27 minutes, or until center is nearly set. Chill 3 hours or longer before serving. If desired, garnish with additional apricot halves.

Makes 6 to 8 servings.

PLAIN PASTRY SHELL

1 cup flour
6 tablespoons butter or margarine, chilled
  and cut into ¼-inch slices
½ teaspoon salt
2 to 3 tablespoons water

1. Place flour in a deep 1-quart bowl. Add butter slices and salt. Using a pastry blender or two knives cut butter into flour until particles are the size of small peas. Sprinkle on water 1 tablespoon at a time, stirring with a fork to gather dough. Form dough into a ball. If possible, wrap in plastic and refrigerate for ½ hour to firm and relax dough.
2. Place ball of dough on a lightly floured work surface. Rolling from the center out, quickly form into a circle 11-inches in diameter. Fold pastry into fourths and place in 9-inch glass pie plate. Unfold and gently maneuver to fit contours of the plate. Fold overhanging pastry maneuver to fit contours of the plate. Fold overhanging pastry underneath to build up a double-thickness rim around the edge. Crimp or flute the rim. Prick the sides and bottom of the shell thoroughly with a fork.
3. Place shell on an inverted saucer or cereal bowl in the oven to elevate. Microwave, uncovered, at power level HIGH for 7½ to 10 minutes, or until pastry looks dry and flaky. Let cool before filling.

Makes 1 9-inch pastry shell.

COOKIE OR GRAHAM CRACKER CRUMB SHELL

6 tablespoons butter or margarine
¼ cup sugar
1½ cups graham cracker or cookie crumbs
  (vanilla wafers, chocolate wafers,
  or ginger snaps)

1. Place butter in a 9-inch glass pie plate. Microwave, uncovered, at power level HIGH for 2½ to 4 minutes, or until melted. Stir in sugar and crumbs. Mix. Press mixture against bottom and sides of pie plate to form crust.
2. Microwave, uncovered, at power level HIGH for 2½ to 4½ minutes, or until set. Let cool before filling.

Makes 1 9-inch crumb crust.

PEACH PIE

2 pounds fresh peaches, peeled and sliced
½ cup packed dark brown sugar
1 tablespoon lemon juice
2 tablespoons cornstarch
⅛ teaspoon ground cinnamon
⅛ teaspoon ground nutmeg or mace
pinch salt

1 9-inch baked pastry shell
 (recipe on page 87)

1. Combine all ingredients, except pastry shell, in a 2 quart mixing bowl. Toss to blend.
2. Turn peaches into pastry shell. cover with wax paper. Microwave at power level HIGH for 13 to 16½ minutes, or until peaches are tender. Serve warm or at room temperature with whipped cream or ice cream.

Makes 1 pie.

PUMPKIN PIE

1 16-ounce can pumpkin
1 14-ounce can sweetened condensed milk
2 eggs
1 teaspoon ground cinnamon
½ teaspoon ground cloves or allspice
½ teaspoon ground nutmeg or mace
1 9-inch baked pastry shell
 (recipe on page 87)

1. Combine all ingredients, except pastry shell, in a 3-quart bowl. Beat until well blended.
2. Pour pumpkin mixture into prepared shell. Microwave, uncovered, at power level LOW & DEFROST for 28½ to 35 minute, or until center is nearly set. Let stand 30 minutes to firm. Chill until serving time.

Makes 1 pie.

MANDARIN CHIFFON PIE

⅓ cup sugar
1 envelope unflavored gelatin
4 eggs, separated
1 11-ounce can mandarin orange sections,
 drained, ⅔ cup syrup reserved
2 tablespoons lemon juice
grated peel of ½ lemon

½ cup sugar
1 9-inch graham cracker or chocolate wafer
 crumb crust (recipe on page 87)

1. In a 1½-quart glass bowl, combine ⅓ cup sugar, gelatin, egg yolks, reserved syrup from oranges, lemon juice, and lemon peel. Beat to blend, Microwave, uncovered, at power level LOW & DEFROST for 6 to 9 minutes, or until gelatin is dissolved, stirring every minute. Be sure not to overheat mixture and scramble the egg yolks; mixture should not come near to boiling. Chill mixture 10 to 15 minutes, stirring occasionally, or until mixture mounds slightly.
2. In a very clean 2-quart bowl, beat egg whites until soft peaks form. Gradually add remaining ½ cup sugar, beating until mixture is stiff and shiny. Fold gelatin mixture and ½ of oranges into beaten egg whites and turn into prepared pie crust. Chill until firm, about 4 hours. Garnish with remaining orange segments.

Makes 1 pie.

CHERRY CORDIAL PIE

3 cups miniature marshmallows
½ cup milk
½ cup maraschino cherries, drained and
 chopped
¼ cup cherry liqueur

1 cup whipping cream, whipped
1 9-inch baked chocolate cookie crumb
 crust (recipe on page 87)

1. Combine marshmallows and milk in a 2½-quart glass mixing bowl. Microwave, uncovered, at power level HIGH for 4 to 5 minutes, or until marshmallows melt and puff. Stir until smooth. Add chopped cherries and liqueur, blending thoroughly. Let cool to room temperature, about 30 minutes.
2. Fold whipped cream into marshmallow mixture and turn filling into prepared pie crust. Refrigerate for at least 4 hours. Garnish, if you wish, with additional whipped cream and maraschino cherry halves.

Makes 1 pie.

CHOCOLATE-ALMOND PIE

6 tablespoons butter or margarine
1 cup dark corn syrup
1 cup slivered almonds, lightly toasted
(about 4 ounces)
⅔ cup sugar
3 eggs
1 tablespoon flour
¼ teaspoon almond extract
½ teaspoon salt

1 9-inch backed cookie crumb crust
(recipe on page 87)
1½ cups semisweet chocolate chips

1. Place butter in a 2-quart glass bowl. Microwave, uncovered, at power level HIGH for 2½ to 4 minutes, or until melted. Add all remaining ingredients, except pie crust and chocolate chips. Beat until smooth. Microwave, uncovered, at power level LOW & DEFROST for 10 to 14½ minutes, or until hot, stirring every 2 minutes.
2. Pour mixture into prepared pie crust. Place pie on an inverted saucer or cereal bowl in the oven to elevate.
Microwave, uncovered, at power level LOW & DEFROST for 7½ to 24 minutes, or until the center is nearly firm. Sprinkle with chocolate chips. Microwave at power level LOW & DEFROST for 1½ to 2½ minutes, or until chips are soft. Remove pie from oven. Using a butter knife, spread softened chocolate chips evenly oven the surface of the pie. Let stand 30 minutes at room temperature. Refrigerate for 2 hours or longer, but remove pie from refrigerator 1 hour prior to serving to soften chocolate top.

Makes 1 pie.

Notes

PUDDINGS AND CUSTARDS, FRUIT DESSERTS

Rich Chocolate Souffle
(Recipe on page 92)

VANILLA CREAM PUDDING

½ cup sugar
2 tablespoons cornstarch
⅛ teaspoon salt
2 cups milk

1 egg, well beaten
2 tablespoons butter or margarine
2 teaspoons vanilla extract

1. In a 1½-quart glass bowl, combine sugar, cornstarch, and salt. Gradually add milk, stirring until completely smooth. Microwave, uncovered, at power level HIGH for 6 to 8 minutes, or until bubbly and thickened, stirring 3 times.
2. In a separate bowl, beat egg with about ⅔ cup of the hot pudding mixture. Quickly stir warmed egg mixture into bowl containing remaining pudding. Microwave, uncovered, at power level HIGH for 2 to 2½ minutes, or until mixture thickens enoungh to coat a spoon, stirring every minute. Add butter and extract, stirring until butter melts. Refrigerate until serving.

Makes 4 servings.

PLUM PUDDING

⅓ cup sugar
¼ cup cornstarch
¼ teaspoon salt
2 cups milk
3 eggs, separated
1 16-ounce can plums, drained, pitted, and
    cut in ½-inch pieces
1 teaspoon vanilla extract
⅛ teaspoon almond extract

1. In a 2-quart glass bowl, combine sugar, cornstarch, and salt. Gradually add milk, stirring until completely smooth. Microwave, uncovered, at power level HIGH for 5½ to 7 minutes, or until bubbly and thickened, stirring 3 times. In a separate bowl, beat egg yolks with about ⅔ cup of the hot pudding mixture. Quickly stir warmed egg yolks into bowl containing remaining pudding. Microwave, uncovered, at power level HIGH for 2 to 2½ minutes, or until mixture thickens enough to coat a spoon, stirring every minute. Fold in plums and extracts. Let cool slightly.
2. In a very clean 2-quart bowl, beat reserved egg whites until fairly stiff peaks form. Fold egg whites into custard. Chill for several hours before serving.

Makes 6 servings.

RICE PUDDING

3 cups milk
½ cup instant rice
1 3-ounce package regular vanilla pudding
    and pie filling
¼ cup raisins
grated peel of ½ orange (optional)
¼ teaspoon ground cinnamon or nutmeg

1. Combine all ingredients in a 2-quart glass bowl or casserole. Cover with wax paper.
2. Microwave at power level LOW & DEFROST for 22 to 25½ minutes, or until pudding is thickened, stirring every 3 minutes. Chill before serving.

Makes 4 to 6 servings.

POTS DE CREME

4 egg yolks
1 teaspoon vanilla
pinch ground cinnamon

1 cup whipping cream
3 squares unsweetened baking chocolate
½ cup sugar
grated peel of ½ lemon (optional)

1. Place egg yolks and vanilla in a 1½-quart mixing bowl and beat with an electric mixer or wire whip until thick and lemon-colored. Set aside.
2. Combine all remaining ingredients in a 4-cup glass measure. Microwave, uncovered, at power level HIGH for 6 to 9 minutes, or until mixture is smooth and quite hot, stirring 3 times. Do not allow to boil.
3. Slowly pour chocolate mixture into egg yolks, beating constantly. Pour mixture into 6 small serving dishes. Chill until firm.

Makes 6 servings.

TAPIOCA PUDDING

2 cups milk
2 eggs, separated
2 tablespoons sugar
2 tablespoons quick-cooking tapioca
1 teaspoon vanilla extract

pinch salt
¼ cup sugar

1. Combine milk, egg yolks, 2 tablespoons sugar, and tapioca in a 4-cup glass measure. Let stand 5 minutes. Microwave, uncovered, at power level HIGH for 10 to 13 minutes, or until pudding comes to a full boil, stirring 4 times. Stir in vanilla.
2. In a very clean 1½-quart mixing bowl, beat egg whites with salt until soft peaks form. Sprinkle on ¼ cup sugar and continue to beat until whites are stiff and shiny. Fold hot tapioca pudding into whites until thoroughly blended. Chill until serving time.

Makes 4 to 6 serving.

EGG CUSTARD

1⅓ cups milk
3 eggs
⅓ cup sugar
grated peel of ½ lemon (optional)
⅔ teaspoon vanilla extract
pinch salt
ground nutmeg

1. Pour milk into 2-cup glass measure and microwave at power level HIGH for 2½ to 4½ minutes, or until scalded. Meanwhile, in a 1½-quart mixing bowl, beat eggs lightly. Add all remaining ingredients, except nutmeg. Quickly stir in scalded milk.
2. Pour custard mixture into 4 well-buttered 6-ounce custard cups. Arrange cups in circle on a glass baking tray. Microwave, uncovered, at power level LOW & DEFROST for 12 to 14 minutes, or until set. Remove cups as they are done and sprinkle with nutmeg to taste. Let cool for 10 minutes at room temperature, then refrigerate until serving time.

Makes 4 servings.

RICH CHOCOLATE SOUFFLE

½ cup sugar
1 envelope plain gelatin
3 eggs, separated
1 cup milk
3 1-ounce squares unsweetened baking
  chocolate, melted

¼ cup sugar
1 cup whipping cream

1. In a 2-quart glass bowl, stir ½ cup sugar and gelatin together. Beat in egg yolks and milk. Microwave, uncovered, at power level LOW & DEFROST for 6 to 7½ minutes, or until mixture has thickened and begun to steam. Stir every minute. Beat in chocolate with a wire whip. Refrigerate until mixture holds it shape softly on a spoon, stirring occasionally.
2. In a very clean 2-quart glass or metal mixing bowl, beat egg whites until soft peaks form. Sprinkle on ¼ cup sugar and continue to beat until whites are stiff and shiny. Fold first the whites, then the whipped cream into the chilled chocolate mixture. Turn into a small souffle dish fitted with a 2-inch paper collar. Refrigerate for at least 4 hours, or until firm. When ready to serve, peel off paper collar and garnish the souffle, if you wish, with additional whipped cream and chocolate curls.

Makes 8 servings.

BAKED APPLES

4 large baking apples
⅓ cup packed dark brown sugar
¼ teaspoon ground cinnamon
⅛ teaspoon ground nutmeg or mace
4 tablespoons butter or margarine
¼ cup dark rum or apple juice or water

1. Core apples, but leave a small piece of the core attached at the base of the blossom end so that the filling will not run out. With a sharp paring knife, cut a hairline circle around the middle of the apple, cutting just deeply enough to go through the skin to the flesh. Arrange apples in a 10-inch round baking dish. Fill cores with brown sugar, sprinkling any excess sugar on top of the apples. Dust tops of the apples with spices. Place 1 tablespoon butter on the top of each apple.
Pour rum into the bottom of the baking dish. Cover.
2. Microwave at power level HIGH for 9 to 13 minutes, or until apples are tender when pierced with a fork. Let stand, covered, 5 minutes before serving. Serve warm or chilled, accompanied by whipping cream, sour cream, or yoghurt.

Makes 4 servings.

RASPBERRY PEARS

½ cup raspberry jam, strained
⅓ cup orange juice
4 pears, peeled, halved, and cored

1 cup sour cream
3 tablespoons raspberry jam
½ cup shaved or slivered almonds, toasted

1. Combine ½ cup strained jam and orange juice in a 10-inch round baking dish. Arrange pears cut-sides-down in dish and spoon some of the sauce over them. Cover. Microwave at power level HIGH for 6 to 10 minutes, or until pears are tender when pierced with a fork. Let stand 3 minutes. Spoon into serving bowl and refrigerate.
2. Swirl remaining 3 tablespoons jam into sour cream. Drop mounds of sour cream mixture onto pears and sprinkle with almonds.

Makes 4 to 8 servings.

STRAWBERRY SHORTCAKE

1 pint fresh strawberries
2 to 4 tablespoons sugar, or to taste

1 cup flour
3 tablespoons sugar
1 teaspoon baking powder
¼ teaspoon salt
4 tablespoons butter or margarine
⅓ cup milk
1 egg

whipped cream

1. Hull strawberries and slice in half lengthwise. Turn into a 1-quart mixing bowl and toss with sugar to taste. Let stand while shortcake is being prepared.
2. Combine flour, sugar, baking powder, and salt in a 1½-quart mixing bowl. Using two knives or a pastry blender, cut in butter until mixture is crumbly. Beat milk and egg together in a small bowl or measure, then pour into flour-butter mixture. Beat vigorously 10 strokes. Turn batter into 4 well-greased-6-ounce custard cups. Microwave, uncovered, at power level LOW & DEFROST for 11 to 14½ minutes, or until cakes are no longer doughy. Let stand for 3 minutes before inverting onto serving plates. Let cool 5 minutes before filling.
3. Split cakes in half crosswise. Spoon strawberries over bottom halves, then cover strawberries with top halves of cakes. Spoon whipped cream on top.

Makes 4 servings.

BLUEBERRY OR CHERRY COBBLER

1 21-ounce can blueberry or cherry pie
  filling
1 teaspoon grated orange peel
¼ teaspoon ground nutmeg or mace

2 cups biscuit mix
½ cup milk
3 tablespoons butter or margarine, softened
2 tablespoons sugar
¼ teaspoon ground cinnamon

1. Combine pie filling, orange peel, and ¼ teaspoon nutmeg in a 1½-quart casserole. Microwave, uncovered, at power level HIGH for 5½ minutes, or until hot, stirring twice.
2. In a 1½-quart mixing bowl, combine all remaining ingredients and beat vigorously 20 strokes. Drop 12 dumplings onto the hot filling. Microwave, uncovered, at power level HIGH for 7 to 10 minutes, or until dumplings are no longer doughy.
Serve warm, accompanied by vanilla ice cream.

Makes 6 servings.

FRUIT COMPOTE

1 cup pitted prunes
1 8-ounce apricot halves, undrained
1 8-ounce can sliced pears, undrained
1 cup sliced peeled apples
1 tablespoon lemon juice
1 tablespoon dark rum or brandy (optional)
¼ teaspoon ground cinnamon
¼ teaspoon ground cloves

1. Combine all ingredients in a 1½-quart glass casserole. Cover.
2. Microwave at power level LOW & DEFROST for 19 to 24 minutes, or until apples are tender, stirring 3 times. Serve warm or chilled.

Makes 4 to 6 servings.

PEACH MELBA

1 16-ounce can peach halves, undrained
1 10-ounce package frozen raspberries, thawed and undrained
½ cup currant jelly
1 tablespoon cornstarch
⅛ teaspoon almond extract

1. Combine all ingredients in a 1½-quart glass casserole.
2. Microwave, uncovered, at power level HIGH for 7½ to 10 minutes, or until mixture is hot and thickened, stirring 3 times. Serve warm over vanilla ice cream.

Makes 4 to 6 servings.

FLAMED FRUIT

1 8-ounce can pitted cherries, drained, syrup reserved
1 11-ounce can mandarin oranges, drained, syrup reserved
1 cup cubed banana
¼ cup sugar
¼ to ½ cup orange juice
¼ cup dark rum or brandy
1 tablespoon lemon juice
1 tablespoon cornstarch

¼ cup dark rum or brandy
vanilla ice cream

1. In a 1½-quart casserole, combine drained cherries, drained mandarin oranges, cubed banana, and sugar. Pour reserved syrups into a 2-cup glass measure. Add ¼ cup rum and lemon juice, plus as much orange juice as necessary to make 1 cup. Beat in cornstarch. Pour syrup mixture over fruit and stir to blend. Microwave, uncovered, at power level HIGH for 6 to 9 minutes, or until sauce is bubbly and thickened, stirring every minute. Turn fruit into serving bowl or chafing dish.
2. Pour remaining ¼ cup rum into a 1-cup glass measure. Microwave, uncovered, at power level HIGH for ½ to 1 minute, or until warm. Pour rum into metal ladle or serving spoon. Ignite. Pour flaming rum over fruit. Spoon fruit over vanilla ice cream.

Makes 6 to 8 servings.

JAMAICAN-STYLE BANANAS

8 tablespoons (1 stick) butter
½ cup packed dark brown sugar
¼ teaspoon ground nutmeg or mace
¼ cup fresh lime juice

4 bananas, peeled
¼ cup dark Jamaican rum

1. Place butter in a 9-inch round glass baking dish. Microwave, uncovered, at power level HIGH for 2½ to 4 minutes, or until melted. Add brown sugar and nutmeg. Microwave, uncovered, at power level HIGH for 4 minutes, or until bubby, stirring every minute. Stir in lime juice. Microwave, uncovered, at power level HIGH for 2½ to 4 minutes, or until sauce looks slightly thickened, stirring every minutes.
2. Place peeled bananas in sauce mixture. Cut in half widthwise and turn in sauce to coat. Microwave, uncovered, at power level HIGH for 4½ to 5½ minutes, or until bananas once. Pour rum into a 1-cup glass measure and microwave, uncovered, at power level HIGH for ½ to 1 minute, or until warm. Pour rum over hot bananas and ignite. Serve at once, accompanied, if desired, with vanilla ice cream.

Makes 4 to 8 servings.

COOKIES & BARS, CANDIES

Best-Ever Almond Bark
(Recipe on page 97)

SUGAR COOKIES

1 cup butter or margarine, softened
1 cup sugar
2 eggs
1 teaspoon vanilla extract
½ teaspoon almond extract
3 cups flour
1 teaspoon cream of tartar
½ teaspoon baking soda
½ teaspoon salt

1. In a 3-quart mixing bowl, cream butter and sugar together until fluffy. Beat in eggs and extracts. Stir in remaining ingredients. Wrap in plastic and chill for at least ½ hour.
2. Roll 1-inch pieces of dough into balls. Place 12 balls on a glass baking tray lined with wax paper. Flatten with the bottom of a drinking glass that has been dipped first in water, then in sugar. Microwave, uncovered, at power lovel LOW & DEFROST for 7 to 10 minutes, or until cookies appear set and dry. Let cool on wax paper. Repeat procedure with remaining dough.

Makes about 36 cookies.

APPLESAUCE FUDGE BROWNIES

8 tablespoons (1 stick) butter or margarine
2 1-ounce squares unsweetened baking chocolate
1 cup packed dark brown sugar
½ cup applesauce
2 eggs
2 teaspoons vanilla extract
1 cup flour
½ teaspoon baking powder
¼ teaspoon baking soda
1 cup chopped walnuts

1. Place butter and chocolate in a 3-quart glass mixing bowl. Microwave, uncovered, at power level HIGH for 2½ to 4 minutes, or until melted. Stir in brown sugar, applesauce, eggs, and vanilla. Blend in flour ¼ cup at a time. Add baking powder and soda. Stir in nuts. Pour batter into a well-greased 8-inch round baking dish.
2. Microwave, uncovered, at power level LOW & DEFROST for 16 to 19 minutes. Cover and let stand 5 minutes, then allow to cool, uncovered. Store in a tightly covered container.

Makes 16 brownies.

RASPBERRY CRUMBLE SQUARES

12 tablespoons butter or margarine, softened
1 cup packed dark brown sugar
1 teaspoon vanilla extract
1¾ cups flour
1½ cups quick-cooking oats
½ teaspoon baking soda
1 teaspoon salt

1 cup raspberry jam

1. Cream butter and brown sugar together in a 2-quart mixing bowl until light and fluffly. Add all remaining ingredients, except jam, and blend thoroughly. Press ½ or mixture into well-buttered 2-quart glass casserole. Microwave, uncovered at power level HIGH for 6½ to 8 minutes, or until mixture looks set.
2. Spread jam evenly over baked layer. Crumble remaining unbaked dough over jam and press lightly with finger tips. Microwave, uncovered, at power level HIGH for 4½ to 6 minutes, or until set. Let cool. Cut into squares.

Makes 9 2½-inch squares.

BEST-EVER ALMOND BARK

1 pound white chocolate
1 cup raisins
1 cup whole almonds

1. Break up chocolate and place in a 2-quart glass mixing bowl. Microwave, uncovered, at power level HIGH for 4½ to 5½ minutes, or until chocolate melts, stirring twice. Stir in raisins and almonds.
2. Immediately pour mixture in a thin layer onto wax paper. Allow to cool thoroughly. Break into pieces.

Makes about 1½ pounds candy.

RUM-RAISIN BARS

¼ cup raisins
⅛ cup dark rum

4 tablespoons (1 stick) butter or margarine
¾ cup graham cracker crumbs
½ 6-ounce package semi-sweet chocolate
  pieces
½ cup chopped walnuts
½ 15-ounce can sweetened condensed milk

1. Combine raisins and rum in a 2-cup glass measure. Microwave, uncovered, at power level HIGH for 1½ minutes, or until mixture is warm. Set aside.
2. Place butter in a 2-quart glass casserole. Microwave, uncovered, at power level HIGH for 1½ to 2½ minutes, or until melted. Add graham cracker crumbs, stir, and press mixture into bottom of dish. Sprinkel chocolate pieces, chopped walnuts, and raisin-rum mixture on top of graham cracker layer. Pour condensed milk evenly over the top.
3. Microwave, uncovered, at power level LOW & DEFROST for 20 to 30 minutes, or until top is lightly browned and center is firm. Let cool to room temperature before cutting into bars.

Makes about 12 bars.

TOFFEE BARS

4 tablespoons (1 stick) butter or margarine
½ cup packed dark brown sugar
¼ cup chopped almonds or hazelnuts,
  highly toasted
5 graham cracker rectangles
½ 6-ounce package semi-sweet chocolate
  pieces

1. Combine butter, brown sugar, and nuts in a 4-cup glass measure. Microwave, uncovered, at power level HIGH for 1 to 2 minutes, or until butter melts. Stir to blend.
2. Place crackers in the bottom of a well-buttered 2-quart glass casserole. Pour butter-brown sugar syrup over crackers. Microwave, uncovered, at power level HIGH for 3 to 4 minutes, or until bubbly and thick-looking. Sprinkle chocolate pieces on top and microwave, uncovered, at power level HIGH an additional 1 to 2 minutes, or until chocolate melts. Spread chocolate evenly over the top. Chill until firm, about 30 minutes. Cut into bars.

Makes about 12 bars.

CHOCOLATE GRANOLA BARS

1 6-ounce package semi-sweet chocolate
  pieces
½ cup peanut butter
3 cups granola (recipe on page 67)

1. Place chocolate pieces in a 2-quart glass bowl. Microwave, uncovered, at power level HIGH for 1 to 2 minutes, or until melted. Stir in peanut butter, blending until smooth. Fold in granola.
2. Turn mixture into a 2-quart glass casserole lined with wax paper. Chill until set, about 1 hour. Cut into bars. Store in refrigerator.

Makes about 20 bars.

BUTTER SCOTCH KRISPIE TREATS

1 6-ounce package butterscotch pieces
3 tablespoons butter or margarine
3 cups miniature marshmallows

3 cups crisp rice cereal

1. Place butterscotch pieces and butter in a 2-quart glass casserole. Microwave, uncovered, at power level HIGH for 2 to 2½ minutes, or until melted. Stir in marshmallows. Microwave, uncovered, at power level HIGH for 1½ to 3 minutes, or until marshmallows are softened, stirring twice. Blend until smooth.
2. Stir rice cereal into marshmallow mixture. Press into casserole. Let stand until cool and set. Cut into squares.

Makes about 16 squares.

S'MORES

8 graham cracker rectangles
1⅛-ounce milk chocolate candy bars
4 marshmallows

1. Top 4 graham crackers with ½ candy bar and 1 marshmallow. Cover with remaining graham crackers. Wrap individually in napkin or paper towel.
2. Arrange cookies on an oven tray with the seam-side of the napkin or towel down. Microwave at power level HIGH for 2 minutes. Let stand 2 minutes before unwrapping and serving.

Makes 4 cookies.

FUDGE

3 cups sugar
12 tablespoons (1½ sticks) butter or
  margarine
1 5-ounce can evaporated milk

1 12-ounce package semi-sweet chocolate
  pieces
2 1-ounce squares unsweetened baking
  chocolate, chopped
1 10-ounce jar marshmallow creme
1 cup chopped nuts
1 teaspoon vanilla
⅛ teaspoon salt

1. Combine sugar, butter, and evaporated milk in a 3-quart glass bowl. Cover with plastic wrap. Microwave at power level HIGH for 13½ to 18 minutes, or until mixture forms a soft ball when dropped in cold water or measures 238°F on a candy thermometer. (Oven should not be in operation when candy thermometer is inserted in fudge.) Stir 2 or 3 times while mixture is heating.
2. Stir in chocolate until melted. Fold in remaining ingredients, blending thoroughly. Turn fudge into a well-buttered large oblong baking dish. Cut when cool.

Makes about 48 1½-inch squares fudge.

PEANUT BRITTLE

2 cups sugar
1 cup light corn syrup
½ cup water

2 cups shelled peanuts, unsalted
2 tablespoons butter or margarine
2 teaspoons vanilla extract
2 teaspoons soda
½ teaspoon salt

1. Combine sugar, corn syrup, and water in a 3-quart glass bowl. Cover with plastic wrap. Microwave at power level HIGH for 22½ to 27 minutes, or until mixture forms threads when dropped in cold water or measures 300°F on a candy thermometer. (Oven should not be in operation when candy thermometer is inserted.) Stir 4 or 5 times while mixture is heating.
2. Stir in all remaining ingredients, blending until smooth. Pour mixture thinly onto two buttered baking sheets. Spread with a knife. Let stand until hard, about ½ hour. Break into pieces.

Makes about 2 pounds candy.

CARAMEL APPLES

1 14-ounce package caramel candy
1 tablespoon water

2 teaspoons butter or margarine, softened
½ cup chopped nuts
6 small apples, stuck with wooden sticks

1. Unwrap candies and combine with water in a 1½-quart glass mixing bowl. Microwave, uncovered, at power level HIGH for 3½ to 4½ minutes, or until melted and smooth, stirring every minute.
2. Spread softened butter on a sheet of wax paper 18 inches long. Sprinkle wax paper with nuts. Dip apples into melted caramel, turning to coat, then place on wax paper, turning to cover with nuts. Let stand 10 minutes to harden.

Makes 6 caramel apples.

Spicy Hot Chocolate
(Recipe on page 101)

SPICY HOT CHOCOLATE

1 cup milk
½ cup sugar
3 1-ounce squares unsweetened baking
  chocolate
1 teaspoon ground cinnamon
¼ teaspoon ground nutmeg or mace
big pinch grojnd cloves or allspice

4 cups milk

1. Place all ingredients, except the last 4 cups milk, in a 3-quart glass bowl. Microwave, uncovered, at power level HIGH for 6 to 9 minutes, or until chocolate melts, stirring twice. Stir until smooth.
2. Gradually blend in remaining milk. Microwave, uncovered, at power level HIGH for 10 to 15 minutes, or until very hot, stirring twice. Be carful that chocolate does not boil over. Ladle into cups and garnish, if you wish, with whipped cream sprinkled with cinnamon, nutmeg, or grated orange peel.

Makes 4 to 6 servings.

IRISH COFFEE

4 cups water
2½ to 3 tablespoons instant coffee
3 tablespoons sugar

½ cup Irish whiskey
½ cup whipping cream, whipped

1. Combine water, instant coffee, and sugar in a 6-cup microwave-safe glass pitcher. Microwave, uncovered, at power level HIGH for 10 to 13 minutes, or until very hot, stirring once.
2. Pour coffee into mugs. Stir in whiskey and top with a dollop of whipped cream.

Makes 6 servings.

ORANGE COFFEE

4 cups water
2½ to 3 tablespoons instant coffee

¾ cup orange liqueur
½ cup whipping cream
2 tablespoons confectioners' sugar
grated peel of 1 orange.

1. Combine water and instand coffee in a 6-cup microwave-safe glass pitcher. Microwave, uncovered, at power HIGH for 10 to 13 minutes, or until very hot, stirring once.
2. Stir orange liqueur into coffee and pour into mugs. Top each mug with a dollop of cream that has been whipped with 2 tablespoons confectioners' sugar. Sprinkle whipped cream with grated orange peel.

Makes 6 servings.

MULLED WINE

4 cups fruity red wine
1 small orange, seeded and thinly sliced
1 small lemon, seeded and thinly sliced
¼ cup packed dark brown sugar
3 cinnamon sticks, broken
3 whole cloves

1. Combine all ingredients in a 2-quart glass bowl.
2. Set microwave oven at power level HIGH for 10 minutes, and then power level LOW & DEFROST for 7½ minutes. Strain into serving mugs.

Makes about 6 servings.

HOT SPICED WINE PUNCH

3 cups apple cider
½ cup packed dark brown sugar
grated peel of 1 orange
grated peel of 1 lemon
3 sticks cinnamon, broken
1 teaspoon whole cloves

1 fifth (3¼ cups)white wine

1. Combine all ingredients except wine in a 3-quart glass mixing bowl. Set microwave oven at power level HIGH for 7½ minutes, and then power level LOW & DEFROST for 13 minutes.
2. Add wine to cider mixture. Microwave, uncovered, at power level LOW & DEFROST for about 8 minutes, or until punch is quite warm. Strain into punch bowl. Garnish with orange slices, if desired.

Makes 6 to 8 servings.

ENGLISH WASSAIL

4 cups apple cider
½ cup lemon juice
½ cup packed dark brown sugar
1 teaspoon whole cloves
½ teaspoon whole allspice
⅛ teaspoon ground nutmeg or mace

1. Combine all ingredients in a 2-quart glass bowl.
2. Set microwave oven at power level HIGH for 10 minutes, and then power level LOW & DEFROST for 10 minutes. Strain into serving mugs.

Makes about 6 servings.

HOT SHERRIED CONSOMME

2 11-ounce cans condensed beef consomme
1 cup water

¼ to ½ cup dry sherry
4 thin, seeded lemon slices
1 tablespoon finely chopped parsley

1. Combine consomme and water in a 1½-quart glass bowl. Microwave uncovered, at power level HIGH for 6 to 9 minutes, or until very hot.
2. Pour consomme into mugs. Stir in sherry to taste and top with lemon slice and chopped parsley.

Makes 4 servings.

HOT APRICOT COCKTAIL

3 cups apricot nectar
½ cup lemon juice
¼ cup packed dark brown sugar
2 cinnamon sticks, broken
1 teaspoon whole cloves

1. Combine all ingredients in a 1½-quart glass bowl.
2. Set microwave oven at power level HIGH for 7½ minutes, and then power level LOW & DEFROST for 10 minutes. Strain into mugs.

Makes about 4 servings.

STRAWBERRY LIQUEUR

1½ pints strawberries, hulled
2 cups sugar
2 cups vodka

1. Place strawberries in a 2½-quart glass bowl and crush lightly with a spoon or mallet. Stir in sugar and vodka. Set microwave oven at power level LOW & DEFROST for 16 minutes, and then power level LOW & DEFROST for 5 minutes.
2. Cover and let stand 3 to 4 days. Strain through a fine sieve lined with washed cheesecloth.

Makes about 2 cups.

PLUM BRANDY

1½ pounds fresh plums, halved and pitted
2 cups sugar
2 cups brandy

1. Combine all ingredients in a 2½-quart glass bowl. Set microwave oven at power level LOW & DEFROST for 16 minutes, and then power level LOW & DEFROST for 5 minutes.

2. Cover and let stand 3 to 4 days. Strain through a fine sieve lined with washed cheesecloth.

Makes about 2 cups.

COFFEE-ORANGE LIQUEUR

1⅔ cups sugar
1½ cups orange juice
⅓ cup instant coffee
2 cups vodka
1 tablespoon vanilla extract

1. Combine all ingredients in a 2-quart glass bowl and stir until coffee is dissolved. Set microwave oven at power level LOW & DEFROST for 12½ minutes, and then power level LOW & DEFROST for 5 minutes.

2. Cover and let stand 3 to 4 days. Strain through a fine sieve lined with washed cheesecloth.

Makes about 2½ cups.

APPENDIX

TABLE FOR HEATING FROZEN CONVENIENCE FOODS

Item	Amount	Power level	Heating time & Comments (in minutes)	
Appetizers (bite size)	2 servings	HIGH	3 to 5	Heat 12 at a time on paper towel lined paper plate or microwave oven roasting rack. Brush pastry items with Worcestershire sauce.
Breakfast Entree	4 to 5 oz	HIGH	2 to 3	If container is ¾-inch deep, remove foil cover and replace foil tray in original box.
Entree	8 to 9 oz	HIGH	7 to 9	For containers more than ¾ inch deep,
	21 oz	HIGH	17 to 19	remove food to similar size glass container; heat, covered if no top crust
Regular TV-style Dinner	11 oz	HIGH	5½ to 8	stir occasionally, if possible.
Hearty TV-style Dinner	17 oz	HIGH	9 to 11½	
Pot pie	8 oz	HIGH	7 to 8½	Brush top of pot pie worcestershire sauce.
Fried chicken	2 pieces	HIGH	4½ to 5½	Arrange on paper towel lined paper plate,
	4 pieces	HIGH	5½ to 7	covered with paper towel.
	6 pieces	HIGH	8 to 9	
Fried fish fillets	2 fillets	HIGH	2½ to 3½	
	4 fillets	HIGH	4 to 5	
Pizzas	1	HIGH	2 to 3	Arrange on microwave oven roasting rack
	2	HIGH	3½ to 4½	
	4	HIGH	5½ to 7	
Pouch Dinners	5 to 6 oz	HIGH	4½ to 5½	Pierce pouch, set on saucer.
	10 to 11 oz	HIGH	8 to 9	
Bagels	2	LOW & DEFROST	2 to 3	Each individually wrapped in paper towel
	4	LOW & DEFROST	3 to 4	(for 1 to 2). Arrange on paper plate, cover with paper towel (for 4 to 6).
Danish	1	LOW & DEFROST	½ to 1	
	2	LOW & DEFROST	1½ to 2	
	4 (6 oz, pkg)	LOW & DEFROST	2½ to 3½	
	6 (13 oz, pkg)	LOW & DEFROST	3½ to 4½	
Dinner rolls	6	LOW & DEFROST	1½ to 2½	
Hard rolls	1 (to 1¼ oz)	LOW & DEFROST	½ to ¾	
	2	LOW & DEFROST	1 to 1½	
	4	LOW & DEFROST	2 to 2½	
Frozen juice Concentrates	6 oz	HIGH	⅓ to 1	Remove lid. If container is foil lined,
	12 oz	HIGH	1 to 3¾	remove to pitcher.
Non-Dairy Creamer	16 oz	LOW & DEFROST	9½ to 10½	Open carton. Let stand equal time after cooking
Pancake	10 oz	LOW & DEFROST	4 to 5	
Whipped Topping	9 oz	LOW & DEFROST	2 to 3	Heat in original plastic tub. Let stand 5 minutes.
Frozen mixed Fruit	10 oz	LOW & DEFROST	4½ to 5½	Pierce pouch or remove metal lid, set on saucer. Let stand 5 minutes.
Frozen vegetable	6 oz	LOW & DEFROST	3 to 4	Pierce box, set on saucer.
	10 oz	LOW & DEFROST	5 to 6	If box foil wrapped, remove foil. If vegetables are in pouch, pierce pouch. Let stand 5 minutes.
Cheese cake	17 oz	LOW & DEFROST	3½ to 4½	Remove from original container arrange on serving plate. Let stand 5 minutes
Brownies	13 oz	LOW & DEFROST	2 to 3	after cooking (to defrost). Add an additional 1 to 2 minutes
Pound cake	10¾ oz	LOW & DEFROST	1 to 2	to serve warmed.
Coffee cake	11 to 12 oz	LOW & DEFROST	3 to 4	

TABLE FOR HEATING

Canned foods	Amount	Power level	Heating time	Standing time
Soup	10½ to 11½ oz.	HIGH	3½ to 7 minutes	3 minutes
Barbecue beef	15 oz.	HIGH	3½ to 4½ minutes	3 minutes
Chicken a la king	12 oz.	HIGH	3½ to 4 minutes	3 minutes
Scalloped tuna	10½ oz.	HIGH	3 to 3½ minutes	3 minutes
Baked beans	8 oz.	HIGH	2 to 3 minutes	3 minutes
Baked beans	15 to 16 oz.	HIGH	4 to minutes	3 minutes
Vegetables	8 oz.	HIGH	2½ to 3½ minutes	3 minutes
Vegetables	16 oz.	HIGH	3½ to 4½ minutes	3 minutes
Sloppy Joe	15 oz.	HIGH	5 to 6 minutes	3 minutes
Ravioli	15 oz.	HIGH	4½ to 5½ minutes	3 minutes
Spanish rice	12 to 15 oz	HIGH	3½ to 5½ minutes	3 minutes

REHEATING TABLE

Item	Amout	Power level	Heating time (in minutes)
Spaghetti sauce	2 cups	HIGH	4 to 5
Soup	1 bowl	HIGH	3 to 4
Beef Stroganoff	2 cups	HIGH	4 to 6
Sliced roast	3 slices	HIGH	1 to 1½
Chicken	3 pieces	HIGH	4 to 5
Fish fillet	1 serving	HIGH	1 to 2
Casserole	1 cup	HIGH	2½ to 4
Lasagna noodle	1 serving	HIGH	4 to 5
Sloppy Joe	1 serving	HIGH	1 to 1½
Mashed potatoes	1 cup	HIGH	2½ to 3½
Bread	1 slice	HIGH	¼ to ½
Dessert	1 serving	HIGH	½ to 1
Baby food	1 jar	HIGH	¾ to 1½
Canned food	2 cups	HIGH	4 to 6

METRIC CONVERSION TABLE

American standard	Metric measure	American standard	Metric measure
1 drop	0.05 mℓ	1 quart	1ℓ
1 teaspoon	5 mℓ	1 gallon	4ℓ
1 tablespoon	15 mℓ	1 ounce	30 grams
½ cup	125 mℓ	1 pound	455 grams (=16oz.)
1 cup	250 mℓ		
1 pint	473 mℓ		

INGREDIENT SUBSTITUTION TABLE

Food	Amount	Substitution
Baking powder	1t.	¼ teaspoon baking soda plus ½ teaspoon cream of tartar
Buttermilk	1 cup	1 cup milk plus 1 tablespoon vinegar or lemon juice
Cake flour	1 cup	¾ cup and 2 tablespoons all-purpose flour plus 2 tablespoons cornstarch
Corn syrup	½ cup	½ cup sugar plus 2 tablespoons water
Fresh herbs	1 t.	⅓ to ½ teaspoon dried herbs
Garlic	1 clove	⅛ teaspoon dried garlic flakes or garlic powder.
Grated fresh fruit peel	1 T.	½ teaspoon dried grated peel
Green pepper	2T. chopped	1 tablespoon dried pepper flakes
Honey	1 cup	1¼ cups sugar plus ¼ cup liquid
Milk	1 cup	½ cup evaporated milk plus ½ cup water ¼ cup nonfat dry milk powder plus 1 cup water and 2 tablespoons butter
Onion	½ cup chopped	1 tablespoon dried onion flakes or 1 teaspoon onion powder.
Unsweetened chocolate	1 oz.	3 tablespoons cocoa plus 1 tablespoon shortening

FREEZER STORAGE TABLE

Food	Storage time at 0°F
Bacon	1 month
Beef, veal, lamb breasts	6 months
Bread	2 months
Cooked dishes	2 to 3 months
Fruit	6 months
Ground meat	1 to 2 months
Juice concentrate	6 months
Pork roasts, chops	3 to 4 months
Poultry	3 to 4 months
Sausage	1 to 2 months
Vegetables	6 months

SERVING AMOUNT TABLE

Food	Amount to buy per serving
Chicken	½ pound
Duckling	2 pounds
Fish steaks, fillets	⅓ pound
Ground meat	¼ pound
Large amount of bone (ribs)	½ to 1 pound
Large dressed fish	½ pound
Medium amount of bone (chuck roast)	⅓ to ½ pound
Rolled turkey roast	⅓ pound
Small amount of bone (steak or roast)	¼ to ⅓ pound
Turkey	½ pound
Whole fish	¾ to 1 pound

INDEX

Notes

Notes

Notes

Printed in Korea.
4891-G 0310-20